Hope for the Muslim Suffering from Anxiety and Panic Attacks

Abby Carlson

This publication is designed to provide accurate and authoritative information about the subject matter covered. It is sold with the understanding that the publisher is not engaged in rendering psychological, financial, legal, or other professional services. This book is not intended as a substitute for consultation or treatment with a qualified mental health professional. If expert assistance or counseling is needed, the services of a competent professional should be sought. Please discuss this with your doctor and only after your doctor's approval you should try the advice given in this book.

In the Name of Allaah,
The Most Merciful,
The Bestower of Mercy

Table of Contents

Chapter 1. Panic - a life-changing experience

I can't pray in a Mosque with many people without an increase in my heart rate.

Whenever on YouTube I see a massive crowd during Hajj, I think about how I am going to do this essential pillar of Islam.

I would give anything if someone promised me twenty-four hours of health and peace in return.

I've had these symptoms for nearly fifty-nine years. Life is very painful for me.

When I see a man limping past my house on crutches I envy him because I feel like I'm much worse off than him.

What are these Muslims talking about?

Why are they so desperate?
What can be so bad that they envy a man who
walks on crutches for his health?

The answer is: They are suffering from anxiety and panic attacks.

We all know what fear is. We become afraid when we have to take an exam or give an important speech, when we make it to the finals in sports, or if we have to go to the dentist. There is a reason for such normal anxiety. But when fear becomes overpowering and overtakes a person for apparently no real reason, then that is something completely different.

Daily life, work, and interpersonal relationships are increasingly affected by these uncomfortable feelings of panic and anxiety that are difficult to control.

Suffering on earth

If those affected with such unreasonable anxiety no longer know how to shake off these agonizing feelings, then that can feel to them like hell on earth, though nothing on earth can be compared to the real Hell which Allah has created for the disbelievers.

People who suffer from anxiety often say that it is impossible to explain to others what they are going through. "It's like trying to talk about color to people who cannot see." The frustrating part is that these sufferers of excessive anxiety had once led a completely normal life. And then one day they had a panic attack. It fell on them like lightning from the blue, and nothing has been the same since. Since then, their everyday life has been determined by the "fear of fear" and they doubt that they will ever be able to lead a normal life again.

One day Salma was standing at the checkout of a supermarket wearing her Hijab and was about to pay the bill. Suddenly her heart began to race and her mouth went completely dry. She could not even recite her Adhkar (remembrance of Allaah). She continued saying the remembrance in her mind. Her hands were shaking so much that she couldn't get her money out of her wallet. She left all the things and fled home. Since then, fear has overwhelmed her every time she went out of the house alone even when she went to the Mosque. She always had to be accompanied by a member of her family. Even today, years after the first attack, she is afraid of going out of the house alone, and she always makes sure that she is never alone in her home.

Helwa worked as a tour guide for women-only groups. She loved her job, but after suffering a panic attack once while traveling she stopped working altogether. She was unemployed for a long time and afterward was only able to take up a relatively undemanding job that did not require her to travel.

Mogahed dearly wanted to be a mother as this is the reason that Muslims marry, but since she suffered from panic attacks, she put off the fulfillment of this wish for so long until it was too late. "I thought I'd never be able to care for a baby."

Hardly any two people experience a panic attack in exactly the same way. Some have unbearable palpitations (uncomfortable awareness of the beating of the heart), others feel dizzy or numb, and still, others get breathless or feel choked. But they all have one thing in common: their life is enormously affected by panic disorders. One fateful day, they had a panic attack. It changed their lives and directed them in a direction that they had not chosen and that they had not wanted. It turned their focus inward instead of outward. It strained their relationships. It became a source of daily fear and worry.

What is a Panic Attack?

We have known panic attacks from literature for centuries.

In 1980 the American Psychiatric Association included the term panic attacks in their Diagnostic and Statistical Manual of Mental Disorders (a reference book for psychotherapists), which is consulted by professionals in diagnosing emotional disorders. The definition given in this reference work is now generally accepted.

The symptoms that are most common during a panic attack are:

- Shortness of breath or breathlessness
- Drowsiness, instability, or weakness
- Palpitations or rapid heartbeat
- Severe tremors
- Sweats
- Choking
- Nausea or "nervous stomach"
- Loss of reality, (depersonalization)
- Numbness or tingling of the limbs
- Hot flashes
- Chest pain or tightness
- Scared to death
- Fear of going crazy or doing something wild!

If most of these symptoms (no matter which) appear at the same time, suddenly and unexpectedly, and if they are clearly and painfully noticeable for a period of about ten minutes, then it is likely to be a panic attack. Also, these symptoms should not be triggered by an obviously life-threatening situation since in such a situation these symptoms are a normal response of the body to the stressful situation.

Many patients experience more than four symptoms; the sensations that accompany a panic attack can also differ slightly from time to time. A certain symptom that a patient suffers from may hardly matter to another. If only one or two of these symptoms are present, it is called a "minor panic attack." Even if a person is faced with one or two of these symptoms frequently and unexpectedly, it can be very worrying and uncomfortable for him or her, and significantly reduce his or her quality of life.

Can I be a normal person if I have panic attacks?

Even if the Diagnostic and Statistical Manual was very useful in that it made a broader professional audience aware of the fact that panic attacks exist, it was of little help in other respects. The reference work coined the expression "panic illnesses" for patients who regularly suffer or fear panic attacks and, so to speak, constantly live with the "fear of fear". It may be useful to give the thing a medical-sounding name, but unfortunately, this gives the impression that the person concerned is suffering from an illness in the true, medical sense. However, this is not the case.

Panic attacks can be fully explained by normal psychological and physiological processes that take place in completely normal people. They can be traced back, for example, to the fact that people had to learn to deal with the stresses and strains of life in an unhealthy way - also to a lack of knowledge about what is going on in their body and to the fear of what might happen to them. Fear and ignorance are common human experiences and have nothing to do with illness.

Can you overcome fear and panic?

Many of those affected by anxiety and panic attacks seek help. Some go to their family doctor and get prescription medication to give them relief. Some are referred to cardiac specialists or neurologists. Some go to a spiritual healer (a *Raaqi*). When one suffers from panic attacks, he thinks that he is suffering from some disease, so he tries to diagnose himself or gets help from his doctor. If a disease is not found he is perplexed and confused. Some seek advice from friends or seek religious help. Some find temporary relief from dangerous *haraam* (illegal) substances such as alcohol and illegal drugs. Others learn how to manage to get on even though they never really get to enjoy life. And with others, nothing seems to work - their life is a constant nightmare.

Can that ever change? Is it possible to get rid of these agonizing feelings? Can life ever be normal again? The answer is yes! Panic doesn't go overnight, but treatment works.

Who is this book for?

It is intended for two target groups:

- It is primarily intended as a self-help book for those affected.

- It is also intended to help relatives, partners, and friends of anxiety patients to understand the problems of their loved ones, and enable them to provide meaningful support to those affected. Most of the time, those taking care of individuals suffering from anxiety also suffer because the phenomenon is so confusing and they never know exactly how to best behave towards those affected. Should they be strict or understanding? Is it a disease or a weakness or just an overreaction?

Those who suffer from this condition often find it helpful to have written material; it can help to deepen the information they have received and to make the treatment more effective.

Can those affected help themselves?

One of the worst side effects of fear and panic is not knowing what is going on.

When those affected by anxiety and panic attacks realize what is really happening, their fear is relieved of much of its horror and they regain hope and confidence.

PROFESSIONAL HELP

Some sufferers need professional help in addition to personal support from friends. Such a person needs to see a clinical psychologist or therapist.

DRUGS

The therapy presented in this book is not based on drug treatment. However, this does not mean that a patient should stop taking the medication that has been prescribed for them.

Nobody should feel guilty about taking medication; on the other hand, a patient should not have the impression that a cure is only possible with the help of medication. The patient can and should decide for himself which path he would like to take. He should discuss the path he chooses with his doctor and listen to his or her advice.

Chapter 2: When and where panic attacks occur

When a person experiences a panic or anxiety attack for the first time, they feel like they have been attacked "like a bolt from the blue" - from one moment to the next and for no apparent reason. They had been a person who, like everyone else, somehow coped with the usual pressures of life, but now he or she suddenly experiences a panic attack, and from that moment on nothing is as it was. The first panic attack almost always begins at a time of suffering and painful change. A person usually experiences their first panic attack between the ages of fifteen and thirty; however, panic attacks can occur at any age.

Patients often use the term "panic" without first hearing it from anyone. Some also see it as a kind of nervous breakdown. They say: "I had a breakdown" and have the feeling that they can no longer do their job. Some feel compelled to give up promising careers.

Unexpected attacks

The most disturbing thing about the first attack is that it comes without warning and that those affected usually cannot see a reason why something so dramatic is happening to them of all people - even if there is always a cause. It is particularly confusing for those affected that they often experience a panic attack when they least expect it, for example during a relaxing weekend or on vacation. If there was a panic attack in a stressful professional or private situation, they might understand the reason for its occurrence.

After the first panic attack, further attacks can occur over the next few days and weeks, and these become a regular part of their everyday life.

Some of the main factors that can trigger panic attacks are:

Certain places

For some people, panic attacks are triggered by being in certain places. These include crowded stores, bus rides, queuing in a store, or just "going into town." This type of panic is technically known as agoraphobia. The expression comes from Greek and means fear (*phobos*) of the marketplace (*agora*). For the people who are affected by this, the feeling of security is tied to a place (usually their home) where they feel safe and secure. They tend to avoid crowds and shops. Sometimes it goes so far that they never leave the house at all.

Certain situations

Some panic when they get into certain situations that make them uncomfortable. For example, excessive anxiety is seen in some when they feel like they are trapped in a room whose exit they cannot see. For these people, security means having an "escape route" in case they get anxious. Others panic when they are bound by time - for example, when they have a doctor's appointment or another fixed appointment. For them, security means avoiding such situations and trying not to commit to anything.

Some panic when they have to do something strenuous on their own. For her, security means doing these things only with her spouse or a good friend or loved one.

Certain feelings

For many people, panic attacks are triggered by certain physical feelings. If you sweat, if your heart is beating faster than usual, or if you feel dizzy, you may have a panic attack. Often these sensations have completely normal causes. However, those affected are not aware of this at the time. They may sweat because the room is too warm, their hearts beat faster because they are on a hike, or they may feel dizzy because they are hungry. Coming from the dark to the light, being exposed to higher air pressure, neon lighting, the surface structure of a floor covering, or a feeling of fullness after eating can trigger unpleasant sensations in certain individuals, and possibly lead to a panic attack.

The flu is also often the cause of panic reactions, as the associated symptoms - drowsiness, sweating, and fever - are very reminiscent of the symptoms of a panic attack. Patients often fail to realize that they just have the flu. For some people, any change in their physical condition triggers panic.

For these people, security means trying to avoid as much as possible the uncomfortable feelings they fear. They keep opening the windows, much to the annoyance of their roommates, so that they don't start sweating. Or they make sure to always walk slowly up the stairs so that their heartbeat does not accelerate. They avoid feeling full by never eating large meals. They are careful and don't do anything that could trigger the dreaded unpleasant feelings. They may also be taking medication for this purpose, such as beta-blockers, which lower the heart rate. To keep the unwanted feelings away they do everything in their power to get rid of them. For example, they lie down very quietly, go out into the fresh air, do relaxation exercises or take medications.

Mental anticipation of certain events

For some people, anxiety begins to build up before they have to do something that they find difficult. Many find themselves in dire straits because a vacation is imminent and the departure date is getting closer. Often the fear of the problem is greater than the problem itself; however, when the dreaded event finally occurs, the patients are already so exhausted that they barely have the strength to deal with the problem on their own and bring their fear under control. These people try to protect themselves by avoiding long-term commitments as much as possible. They prefer to make spontaneous decisions. If they feel that a panic attack is approaching, they even decide to cancel a vacation trip, even if it is financially expensive and a big loss. Then there is the embarrassing feeling of lying to others or having to put forward reasons in order to wriggle out of commitments that have already been made.

Certain actions

Certain things a person does can trigger panic attacks. They can occur while resting, overhearing an argument, or running upstairs. For these people, security means doing something that helps them - may be lying down or sitting down, running in place, tensing their muscles, or taking a few deep breaths. For them, safety can also mean consciously avoiding certain things - not relaxing, not reading certain newspaper articles, and not participating in conversations about certain topics (e.g. mental illness or heart attack).

WATCHING TV

Hameed was just sitting on the sofa watching TV. Then he suddenly noticed that his heart was beating fast. It was getting worse and worse. The fear rose in him like a hot wave. He felt like this whenever he heard someone talking about a heart attack.

Thinking about panic

In some people, just thinking about panic attack, or hearing or reading something about it can trigger a panic attack.

It is quite difficult to control our thoughts, but many of these people try to keep the thought of panic attacks away by distracting themselves, keeping themselves busy, and never allowing themselves to relax.

Sleep

Another factor that can trigger panic attacks is sleep. When falling asleep, some people have the frightening impression that their heart is beating at breakneck speed, that they are falling into the abyss, losing consciousness, or the like. Others wake up sweating with a jerky movement; their hearts are pounding and they are gasping for air. Others feel paralyzed when they wake up. This state usually only lasts a few moments - but to those affected, it seems like an eternity.

More often than not, people who deal with this type of panic try to avoid what triggers the scary feelings.

For them, safety means preventing oneself from falling asleep, staying awake until it gets light, or sleeping in a semi-sitting position. Some make sure that all "dangers" are largely eliminated when they want to fall asleep - they make sure that someone sleeps with them, or that they have a few tablets or at least the phone next to them "just in case". Sleeping pills, milk with honey, or the like are often used as sleep aids.

Phobias

Phobias (irrational fears) are common. There are many different types of phobias, such as fear of insects or other specific animals, fear of heights, fear of water, vomiting, blood, hospitals, dentists, or fear of being with other people and having to talk to them.

If someone has a phobia, there is almost 100% certainty that a panic attack will be triggered if they are confronted with what they fear.

The problem is very specific and predictable - under normal circumstances, people behave fairly normally, but panic as soon as they come into contact with the dreaded object or get into the dreaded situation.

Panic attacks are less predictable than phobic reactions and are not triggered by a very specific "trigger", that is a triggering stimulus. The dreaded objects are not outside, but inside their own personality - the person concerned is not afraid of spiders, dogs, or bridges, but of their own feelings and physical reactions.

Chapter 3: How panic attack changes people

A hurricane may only last a day, but the aftermath can still be felt weeks and months later. It's the same with panic. After the panic attack itself is over, the person concerned is preoccupied with it for a long time. Let's take a look at the typical response patterns that follow a panic attack.

First step: Fear becomes a constant companion

The first thing that happens is that the person becomes very afraid of having another panic attack and is afraid of what might happen during a possible next attack. A feeling of impending disaster creeps up on him and takes hold of him more and more. Some patients get really scared after two or three attacks, others do after just one attack. While their life was quite normal before, with the usual ups and downs, fear is now all-pervading and also limits those affected such that they are no longer able to enjoy the little joys in life that they were able to enjoy until then.

Second step: The attention is directed inwards

Second, people suffering from panic attacks tend to turn their attention away from what is happening around them. They are not mindful. They can no longer concentrate properly on what others are saying or doing because they are constantly preoccupied with their own feelings. It is as if a person's gaze is averted from the outer world and only fixed on what is going on inside him.

Those affected begin to consciously register everything that happens in their body - they develop, so to speak, a completely new "body awareness". They notice when their heartbeat is accelerating and frequently measure their pulse. They were smartwatches to monitor their pulse and temperature. They will immediately notice when they start to sweat, breathe faster than usual, and when feeling a little nauseous. Every few hours they check that everything in their body is still working properly. Every physical sensation that reminds them remotely of what they experienced during a panic situation they register immediately because their fear of suffering another attack is so overwhelming.

The problem with this is that our bodies are constantly changing. When we make an effort, for example when we walk or run fast, our heart beats faster than usual, and that is completely normal. But for someone who is constantly watching himself/herself, this can be a cause for concern. People can be overly sensitive to just a specific or a whole range of sensations.

In summary, it can be said that these people are:

- unconsciously constantly directing their attention to the feelings that are most uncomfortable for them,

- react extremely sensitively to even the smallest emotional fluctuations,

- perceive their own sensations immediately,

- concentrate fully on their own feelings as soon as they notice them.

Third step: The fear of certain feelings

Thirdly, those affected become afraid of certain feelings. If they believe that a panic attack was really a heart attack, then the symptoms they fear most are a faster heartbeat, chest pain, sweating, or palpitations. As soon as they experience any of these symptoms, they become anxious.

Those affected can be afraid not only of certain physical sensations but also of certain thoughts. For example, they might think, "I'm going crazy," and that thought that goes through their heads over and over again and it really scares them.

Fourth step: the vicious circle

Fourth - and this is one of the main reasons why panic attacks often recur - those affected get into a vicious circle. You may notice some changes in your physical condition, such as an increase in your heart rate. If you fear a panic attack is occurring, that fear can make your physical symptoms worse. The heart beats even faster - the fear increases even more, and this can make the heartbeat even faster. So, the fear of a panic attack can actually trigger one. This phenomenon is often mentioned in specialist literature. One finds the terms "fear of fear", "symptom anxiety", "anxiety spiral" or "panic spiral".

Step five: avoidance patterns

Fifth, those affected begin to change their lifestyle. They avoid places where they once had a panic attack and are careful not to put themselves in a situation that they fear could trigger an attack on them. They try hard not to do anything or think anything that could lead to a panic attack.

Complete avoidance

A person can be affected so badly by panic attacks and agoraphobia that he may not be able to leave his house at all.

Individual avoidance strategies

There are many strategies that those affected use to ward off a feared panic attack as it develops. Some typical behavior patterns are:

- take medications to control your heart rate or sweating before a task that is perceived as difficult,

- take along a good friend with you,

- hold a child by the hand,

- bring a dog or a walking stick,

- chew gum or suck candy,

- stay constantly tense inside,

- wear sunglasses,

- constantly busy yourself with something,

- always stand close to a wall and/or a door,

- only tackle things on "good days",

- Constantly encouraging yourself with positive thoughts like "you will do it, you will do it".

Some therapists refer to these strategies as magic: as long as the person concerned carries the "magical" object with him or carries out the "magical" act, he feels safe. People suffering from panic attacks are extremely inventive in developing avoidance strategies. As one patient put it:

Going shopping requires just as much careful preparation as robbing a bank. You have to plan every step carefully, and as long as there is an escape route at all times, shopping is usually manageable.

Being prepared for the worst (having "lifesavers" with you)

You could describe this strategy as follows: always have a first aid kit with you in order to be prepared in the event of an accident. There are many different methods to get around at least to some extent to keep the fear in check if it makes itself felt. Some people always have something with them that makes them feel like they are equipped for an emergency - a flask in their handbag, a self-help book for panic patients, or a cell phone.

Many of those affected always have a couple of tranquilizers in their pockets, "just in case". The feeling of being able to take a tablet in an emergency is often enough to give the person concerned a feeling of security.

Many patients have acquired a whole "arsenal" which they fall back on in order to be able to keep the fear at a tolerable level in an emergency - they lie on the bed, take a few deep breaths, drink water, take tranquilizers, trying to reassure yourself, go jogging, or simply try to ignore their physical symptoms.

Avoidance strategies: "Live now, pay later"

Although it seems obvious that avoidance strategies are a useful means of preventing feelings of panic or at least reducing them to a manageable level, they only offer temporary relief. In the long run, on the contrary, they only ensure that the underlying problem persists.

Those affected may feel that they are pouring water on the fire and thereby putting it out; however, they are holding the wrong canister and are really just pouring oil on the fire. Avoidance strategies have a destructive effect in the long term, because

- they restrict the lives of those affected and their room for maneuvering more and more; their quality of life decreases noticeably;

- they make the patient unable to cope with a really severe panic attack (if it indeed comes to that extent) because they have only learned to deal with the symptoms of panic attacks and not with the actual condition;

- it prevents those affected from realizing the truth namely what would happen if they no longer tried to avoid, stop or alleviate panic attacks.

What would happen if you stopped trying to fight panic? This notion may be frightening at first, but precisely this - giving up the fight - is an important key to successful therapy.

Chapter 4: What is a panic attack?

The human body works in amazing ways. Everything seems to be specially created to keep us alive and to protect us from harm. Take, for example, a cut on your finger - why doesn't the blood keep flowing out of the wound until you have bled to death? The body recognizes that we have cut ourselves and reacts to the changed situation. When the blood comes into contact with air, it begins to clot. It clumps together, gets thicker and thicker, and forms a crust. After a few days, this will fall off and the whole thing will be forgotten. The whole thing works like clockwork. Regardless of whether we are awake or asleep, whether we are stupid or clever - the body heals itself, automatically.

What happens if we choke - if we accidentally get food or drink down our windpipe? We start coughing and gagging automatically, and in this way, the foreign body is thrown out of the windpipe again. We don't think: "Eating in the windpipe is dangerous, I have to cough it up again" - our body does this for us and automatically does the right thing.

What happens when we eat something that is already bad or poisonous? The stomach realizes that something is wrong and pushes the food back up. We feel sick, we throw up - it is not very pleasant, but it serves the purpose - and our body has rid itself of the unsuitable food.

When we get a contagious disease, such as the flu, our body identifies the pathogen and produces antibodies whose task is to isolate the pathogen and render it harmless. With every new disease we get, our body also produces new antibodies. The next time we get infected with the same pathogen, the antibodies act immediately and the disease cannot break out in the first place. The way antibodies work is so complex that there is still something new to discover in the field, even though science has been deeply involved in the subject for many years. Yet the smallest child can produce antibodies without giving a single thought. Millions of cells are in action day and night to protect us, and the most amazing thing is - it all happens by itself.

These were just four examples of how our body takes care of us - but it has an almost inexhaustible repertoire of ways to protect us. A hundred modern computers couldn't take care of us half as well as our own bodies. Our body has amazing protective mechanisms that it uses for us at all times.

The fear response

One of the automatic protective mechanisms of our body is the fear response. Imagine the following situation: We are walking down a narrow, tree-covered street. Suddenly two Rottweilers jump toward us, growling and barking. They bare their teeth furiously. Drool runs out of her mouth. Before acting do we think, "This is a dog. He growls. He snaps at my hand. I am in danger. I should do something now to protect myself. What could I do? Maybe I should run away. Yeah, I think that would be the best. I'm running away now!" No, that's not how we react. If we do that we'd probably be mangled before we'd finished our thought process.

No, our body reacts instinctively and with lightning speed. There is adrenaline pumping, our heart pounding, we break into a sweat, and before we can even think we are either on the run or fighting like mad with the dogs. That is the fear response. It is there to protect us from harm.

Suppose we run away: the dogs are right behind us, they growl angrily and snap at us. But we are very fast, we manage to escape them. After about a hundred meters we have the feeling that we are far enough away to be able to turn around.

If we now consciously turn to our bodies, what do we notice?

- Our heart is beating like the engine of a diesel locomotive, fast and powerful.

- We breathe very quickly and deeply.

- We sweat and shiver all over our bodies.

- Our mouths are completely dry.

- We feel sick and dizzy.

- We feel a tingling sensation in our hands and feet.

- We are inwardly troubled, tense, and vigilant; we expect to be in danger again.

Are we scared? Well, the dogs scared us, but now they seem to have calmed down and only bark in the distance. But the physical changes that we feel do not scare us, even if they are very evident and very strong. They don't worry us because we know where they come from. They are an integral part of our fear response. They'll go away in a few minutes. They don't frighten us because we know their cause. The fear response is there to protect us. If someone had recorded our 100-meter sprint, we would find that we had run personal bests. The fear reaction releases additional forces in us that we need to escape danger.

The fear response is at the heart of a panic attack. The symptoms that accompany the anxiety response and the panic attack are identical - faster heartbeat, faster breathing, sweating, tremors, dry mouth, tingling in the hands and feet, and so on. A panic attack doesn't always have to have all of these symptoms appear at the same time, and not all patients feel the same - but in principle, it can be said that the anxiety response and the panic attack are essentially the same. The only difference - and this is a huge difference - is that the fear response has an obvious reason (e.g., we are being attacked by angry dogs) and the panic attack does not.

There is no obvious cause for a panic attack like a growling dog or a human attacker causing severe symptoms in us. No wonder people who suffer panic attacks are often completely at a loss. They cannot see the reason for their strong feelings. They think they have a heart attack or a brain tumor, a nervous breakdown, or they have lost control of themselves. The fear response is so strong that the person concerned thinks there must be a solid reason or a medical disease for their feelings. Most people who were faced with emotions like this out of the blue would be seriously concerned and suspect that something really bad is happening. It is perfectly normal to think that way.

The truth is, however, that when you have a panic attack, the body's normal fear response is triggered accidentally.

The fear reaction "from head to toe"

Our bodies are made to protect us. Every single component of the fear response has a very specific reason, namely to ensure our survival. None of these symptoms harm us - on the contrary, they are there for our protection. It's basically the same with panic. None of the symptoms can harm us.

HEART SYMPTOMS

Waves of fear rolled through my body. I knew I couldn't get through this time, this time I was going to die. I gasped and my heart was pounding like crazy. I put my hand on it so I could feel it. It was beating very quickly.

Panic and anxiety usually include an acceleration in the heart rate. Eighty-five percent of those affected report that their heart pounds violently during a panic attack. For some patients, the fact that they can clearly feel their own heartbeat during an attack even becomes a major problem. The heart beats faster than usual, and those affected often have the impression that it is beating more vigorously. Sometimes it hits irregularly or skips a beat. Some people feel the blood pulsing in their veins on the back of their necks. Often there is pain and pressure in the chest. Some people feel like their heart is beating very quickly when they fall asleep, and others wake up with this feeling in the middle of the night.

What good can it do to us if our heartbeat speeds up? The heart is of vital importance to us because it pumps the fresh arterial blood and the vital oxygen it contains into our body, into the most remote areas, and right into the outermost layers of our skin. Our whole body depends on oxygen. If we have to fight like a lion or run away like an oiled lightning bolt, then the most important parts of the body - in this case our arms and legs - need to be optimally oxygenated as quickly as possible. For that to happen, our heart has to beat much faster than usual.

Gastrointestinal tract symptoms:

I get this weird feeling in my stomach and all I want to do is run away ... well ... it's a very weird feeling, you know.

When a person is in danger, digestion is of secondary importance. The blood is drawn from the less important parts of the body (in this case the gastrointestinal tract) and fed to the more important parts of the body (the arm and leg muscles) so that we can run away quickly (or fight well). This can cause a feeling of nausea - butterflies in your stomach - or a growl in your stomach. The bladder and bowel are preparing to empty and we feel like we need to go to the bathroom urgently. (However, it almost never happens that people spontaneously empty their bladders during a panic attack.)

SKIN SYMPTOMS

Blood is drawn from the skin, fingers, and toes so it can flow to the arms and legs. We become pale and feel like we are losing blood, or we feel tingling or numbness in the outer areas of our body. It is good for us to reduce the blood supply to the skin - not only so that our muscles can get a better blood supply, but also so that we don't lose as much blood when we are injured.

BREATHING

I could hardly breathe and then these strange feelings started in my stomach. It was terrible to be unable to breathe properly - I gasped for air and then I realized that the street and the houses looked very strange.

When we panic, our breathing becomes faster and deeper. This is done so that a lot of oxygen gets into the lungs. Through the lungs, which are surrounded by blood vessels, the oxygen then enters the bloodstream and from there to the muscles. Since the muscles receive a particularly large amount of oxygen during a panic attack, the breathing rate accelerates and this can lead to shortness of breath or feelings of suffocation. Fifty-three percent of panic patients say they suffer from shortness of breath during a panic attack and forty-eight percent from feelings of suffocation. The chest hardens and this leads to a feeling of tightness or heaviness in the chest. Some people feel that they are not getting enough air and try their best to draw more air into their lungs. If the oxygen we breathe is not used up by the effort of fighting or running away, symptoms occur such as tingling in the fingers and toes, dizziness, or the feeling of "not being there" and losing the ground beneath your feet. If we are afraid of not getting enough air and therefore breathe even deeper and harder, then we take in more oxygen than we need.

How does this help us in a dangerous, fear-inducing situation? When we have to run away quickly, our body needs as much oxygen as possible. Deep, quick breathing ensures that we get it. You can sometimes see that athletes take a few deep breaths before a race so that their body is optimally supplied with oxygen for the upcoming exertion.

TREMBLE

... I went to a sports club to play but I couldn't concentrate at all. My hands started shaking. "Pull yourself together man", I said to myself. But my hands continued shaking, and my whole body ...

Seventy percent of panic patients report trembling violently during an attack. This can be attributed to the increased adrenaline level and the strong arousal. The tremor is a sign that those affected have enough energy and tension to face the danger. However, since they lack the opportunity to convert this energy and tension in a suitable way or to let it flow away, they begin to tremble violently.

When we're not running away or fighting, we have more oxygen in our arms and legs than we can use. This makes us shiver, or we get weak knees or "rubber legs". If we sit still, we have a very uncomfortable feeling because we are not using up the energy that nature has provided us with.

SWEAT

Our glands are also affected by the fear response. We sweat or alternate between hot and cold so that our bodies don't overheat. It works just like a thermostat. Many patients with panic attack have profuse sweating during an attack. The salivary glands in our mouth dry up and we get dry mouths. Sometimes people report having a strange taste in their mouth, such as a metallic or peppermint-like taste. Others find that their bodies emit a special odor during a panic attack.

SENSATION OF TENSION, SENSATION OF CHOKING, AND SWALLOWING SYMPTOMS

Sometimes certain muscle groups become tense, for example, the arm and leg muscles or the abdominal muscles, the neck muscles, or the chest muscles. If the muscles of the anterior neck area tighten, the salivary glands dry out, and the patient is breathing heavily and deeply at the same time, then it is common (in sixty-one percent of patients) to experience suffocation or difficulty swallowing.

The increased muscle tone can cause involuntary twitching or tremors. When we have to fight or flee, our bodies have to be tense. When we're running for our lives, we don't need to eat at the same time. So it doesn't matter if our mouth is dry because saliva is mainly produced so that we can chew and swallow our food better.

HEAD AND EYE SYMPTOMS

Patients also complain of dizziness and impaired balance. They often hold on to something for fear of falling over.

Some may have blurred or distorted vision during an attack; others complain that they can read poorly, especially when they are close to something.

In the fear reaction, the pupils open wide (this is due to the increased adrenaline level). As a result, more light flows into the inside of the eye, and this serves to ensure that as much of the environment is perceived as possible so that you can clearly see the impending danger. The muscles that focus the eye also tense and adjust the focus so that you can see things between three and ten meters away particularly well. This is very useful when you are in battle or fighting wild animals (but not when you work in an office and are trying to read and write). The unconscious control mechanisms of the human body seem to be programmed in such a way that they ensure optimal vision at a medium distance in a dangerous situation.

OVER-SENSITIVITY

I became overly sensitive, and couldn't stand any noise or touch. Not even that the TV was on. I couldn't bear to feel the sheets on my bed - not even the hair on my head.

When we are very afraid, we are much more vigilant than usual and are much more sensitive to light and sound. Just the ringing of the phone makes us jump. When we are so sensitive, we often react very irritably to the people around us.

Sometimes people in a panic situation have a terrible feeling that something horrific, and ominous is about to happen. Since the fear reaction is about recognizing danger and avoiding death and injury, it is not surprising that those affected in this situation also have premonitions of impending disaster and destruction. Add to this the fear of what terrible might happen to you during the panic attack.

LOSS OF CONCENTRATION

I try to focus on the conversation that is going on because when you're so busy with yourself you tend to drift away internally. You're drifting into your own little world - how you feel, how fast your heart beats, and all that.

It is very difficult for people to focus on things like reading or talking because they spend so much energy dealing with their physical symptoms.

During a panic attack, some also have the impression that they cannot control their thoughts, that they can no longer make well-considered decisions, and that their thoughts seem to be overturning. This is not surprising, because the fear response makes us extremely alert and accelerates many of our physical functions - including our minds. We must concentrate our full attention on where the danger threatens us and how we can escape it, and we cannot afford to think long and make well-considered decisions. Our minds also seem to switch to danger mode, so to speak - away with all the intellectual stuff!

LOSS OF REALITY

Fifteen to twenty percent of those affected suffer from feelings of loss of reality or "depersonalization". They feel that the world around them is unreal or strange, or that they have become a different person. Such experiences can be very frightening and undermine a person's self-confidence.

Is the fear response dangerous?

Many people who have panic attacks feel that the symptoms are dangerous because they are so severe.

But what is the point of having an "automatic" fear response if it were to harm us? The fantastic protective mechanism that saves us from being torn apart by an angry lion will not kill us after we have escaped to safety. That wouldn't make any sense. Yes, the symptoms are very strong - they have to be if they are to help us to escape a dangerous situation.

Secondary reactions to panic attacks

Some feelings are not part of the fear response, but they do occur as a consequence. Often, people who experience very frequent panic attacks experience feelings of powerlessness and despair. When panic attacks suddenly hit a person and ruin their previous life, it is all too understandable that they are convinced that there is no longer any hope for them. The following three secondary reactions are particularly common.

Obsessive thoughts

Obsessive-compulsive thoughts can be very depressing and debilitating. They come without the person concerned wanting it. They are the exact opposite of what he would like to think. They are often directed against what the person concerned loves most or what is most precious to him. For example, a mother who loves her baby is tormented by the idea of stabbing or strangling it. She naturally finds such thoughts terrible. Or a loving husband has the recurring thought of harming his wife. Some patients have an obsession with doing something stupid that will ruin their careers. Such thoughts are always accompanied by strong emotions, and those who suffer from them often fear that these obsessions may one day become so strong that they may act. But these are just thoughts and imaginations.

People who fear these obsessive-compulsive thoughts often try to forcibly banish them. The reality, however, is that by giving these thoughts so much attention they make them all the more powerful.

FORGETFULNESS

Forgetfulness is also a factor that many anxiety patients complain about. People often think that their forgetfulness is a sign that they are losing their minds. In reality, however, part of the forgetfulness comes from being so preoccupied with their problems and symptoms that the concerns of daily life become less important.

EXHAUSTION

If you are constantly faced with this terrible fear, it takes all your strength away. The daily tasks then seem to take on gigantic proportions; Putting a basket of laundry into the machine can then be an almost insolvable problem.

The person concerned has to use all his strength to fight panic feelings and to resist them. It is becoming more and more difficult for him to cope with his daily life.

Please take my fear away!

Panic sufferers often wish that all of these uncomfortable feelings would just go away, once and for all, or that someone could get them out of them like a surgeon removes a cancerous sore. However, getting rid of our fear response would likely mean losing our lives.

The physical symptoms are perfectly natural and harmless as such - although they can be very frightening to a person who cannot tell what caused them.

Chapter 5. What panic is not

In essence, fear is based on the belief that danger is imminent. One who has a panic attack may think they are going to have a heart attack and the other may think they are crazy or have a nervous breakdown. The thought of impending danger is pervasive, but different people imagine different types of danger during a panic attack.

Panic is not what it appears to be

Sometimes we are wrong. Take a man in a train station. It was rush hour. The subway pulled in. It was completely full; people were standing close together. But he thought he might still squeeze in and tried it. As he stood with his back to the door and waited for it to close, to his great surprise another person pushed himself into the car and stood behind him. At the same moment, he felt a cold piece of steel dig into his back. He'd heard a lot about robbery and violence in the subway. Should he be killed now? Would the stranger ask him to give him his wallet? There was a cold sweat on his forehead. He started to tremble. He gathered all his strength and turned slowly, ready to face the culprit, expecting the knife to pierce his back at any moment. And then ... he couldn't believe his eyes. Behind him stood a little old lady with an umbrella under her arm, and what he had felt in his back was the tip of that umbrella! He was wrong.

As long as the man believed that a thief with a knife was standing behind him, he was sweating and shaking, and his heart was racing - he was scared. But when he saw the little old lady his feelings changed at once; he was relieved and thought he had been really stupid to believe such nonsense.

A panic attack is basically something like that old lady with an umbrella - terrifying until you know what it is, but completely harmless once you know it.

But a panic attack is such a terrible experience!

Yes, panic attacks are very scary. Yes, the feelings are very, very strong. Yes, they seem to attack you for no reason, like lightning from the blue. Yes, those affected have a strong desire to do something so that "it" doesn't happen again. But - panic attacks are not what they appear to be. They don't cause a nervous breakdown, a stroke, or a heart attack. You don't lose control of yourself, you don't faint, and you don't make a fool of yourself. It feels like something like this has to happen, but it doesn't happen.

Misconception No. 1: "It never stops"

One particularly widespread fear is that panic will never stop on its own. Feelings of panic arise suddenly and get stronger and stronger until those affected do something to get rid of them. Maybe they quickly leave the supermarket when that is the place where their fear is greatest, maybe they sit or lie down, maybe they distract themselves, call the doctor or take tranquilizers - whatever will make the fear subside. When they have calmed down again, they have the impression that the attack continued and that at its climax the dreaded bad event would have occurred if they had not intervened and done something about it. But those affected only think

Some bare facts

Our body itself ensures that a panic attack is short-lived and a person recovers in a few minutes. In a small number of patients whose panic attacks lasted over half an hour, the main cause for the long duration was due to their efforts to fight the panic attack. They tried to suppress, stop or analyze the panic attacks. However, such efforts only result in an attack taking longer than it normally would; they also cost a lot of strength. If, on the other hand, you "endure" a panic attack, so to speak, without fighting it, then it can take its normal course. Claire Weekes, who has written some of the best books on anxiety makes the following comparison:

"If we allow a panic attack, then we are, as it were, allowing a wave to take hold of us and take us with it, instead of us trying to swim against it."

Having a panic attack is like crying in many ways. Imagine a colleague or friend has died. You may feel like crying when you're alone in your apartment in the evening thinking about it. This is completely normal. If you allow yourself to cry, you may cry for a few minutes or a little longer. If you allow yourself to express your pain, it will pass. If you let things take their course, they will take care of themselves. And what happens when you fight the pain and try to hold back your tears? You may succeed for a while, but then the desire to cry comes back. You fight it again - it stops but soon it will be back. In this way, the desire to cry lasts for many hours. In other words, when you struggle against your feelings, they keep coming back; if you allow your feelings to run their normal course, then they will pass much faster. It's the same with panic.

Chapter 6: Wrong beliefs about death and disease

Misconception: "It's my heart"

I'm having a heart attack. This time it's a difficult one. I'm going to die from this heart attack.

Panic attacks are reminiscent of heart attacks in many ways. Heart attacks also lead to palpitations, chest pain, sweats, and shortness of breath. In the past, panic attacks were also known as "cardiac neuroses" because their symptoms are similar to those of heart disease. After their first panic attack, those affected often call their family doctor, who then comes by and examines them. To the great astonishment of the patient, the doctor usually cannot find anything unusual. Your condition is not indicative of a heart attack. But the diagnosis "You are all right" is of course very unsatisfactory for someone who has just experienced such a terrible attack. In order to satisfy the patient, or to be on the safe side, the general practitioner may refer him to a heart specialist.

It will of course take some time for the patient to get an appointment; then the usual tests are done, and finally, the cardiologist tells the family doctor that there is no heart disease - the patient may have mild arrhythmias (the heart "skips" a beat every now and then) or slightly elevated EKG (or ECG) values, but nothing that is clinically significant. The doctor then tells his patient that the EKG values are slightly increased, but that he is clinically perfectly healthy.

The patient may go home feeling that he is really seriously ill, that the doctors have overlooked something, that they are not competent, or that they are hiding something, and they may still think they have a heart condition. A panic patient who is considered to be in perfect health simply doesn't know what to think of it. It felt just like a heart attack - and if it wasn't, what was it?

"It all only happens in the head" - unfortunately, this phrase is often used in connection with fear. Those affected often think that this means: "You are just imagining it." They try to convince themselves that they are only imagining these panic attacks, and they often doubt their own sanity. The symptoms were so real - my heart was beating like crazy, and I could hardly breathe - how can I have imagined it all?

Of course, the symptoms are real - fever, sweats, accelerated heartbeat, all of these symptoms are real and can be clearly diagnosed. Instead of "it all only happens in the head", it would be better to say: "This has psychological causes" or "This is a psychosomatic problem." The symptoms of a panic attack are physical and very real; however, they have emotional causes and are not the result of physical illness.

How can you tell if it's a heart attack or a panic attack? In both cases, the patient has chest pain, his heart beats significantly faster than usual, and he suffers from shortness of breath.

When these symptoms occur in certain situations (for example, when we rest in the evening, when we have to wait in line, when we think about our problems, when we have argued at home) or in certain places (in shops, buses, elevators, in a religious place, or at the hairdresser's), then it is probably a panic attack, not a heart attack. Panic is always tied to certain triggers (even if we may not know them all). In contrast, heart attacks are not so closely related to certain triggering situations or events.

There is an exception to this rule. The symptoms of heart disease can get worse the more you physically exert yourself. Panic attacks can also occur during physical exertion, but they usually occur on other occasions as well. When we exert ourselves, for example when we climb a flight of stairs or when we walk relatively fast on a cold morning, it is only normal for our heart to beat faster and our breathing to get faster and deeper. However, if this is the only situation where someone experiences chest pain, then they should seek medical advice because they may really have heart disease. "Chest pain" means pressure or heaviness behind the sternum, or pain or burning between the shoulder blades, sometimes in the neck or jaw.

You should always rely on your doctor's judgment more than on your own.

Misconception: "I will die"

Some people fear that their panic attacks, which are so powerful and trigger such strong feelings, will in the long run be physically or mentally harmed - that the Attacks could trigger a heart attack or stroke, for example. But the human body seems to survive panic attacks very well, again and again, and for a long period of time. The substances released into the bloodstream during a panic attack, including adrenaline, are produced by the body and basically work to protect it, not to harm it. Claire Weekes in her book Peace from Nervous Suffering says: "If you knew how thick and how strong is your heart muscle, then you would lose all fear that it would tear through faster or stronger beating or could be damaged." The same goes for a severe headache. Even if you can clearly feel the blood pulsing in the veins, it does not burst and cannot cause a cerebral hemorrhage or brain tumor.

Even if it is impossible to die from a panic attack, it can happen that someone who has previously suffered from a physical illness (such as a weak heart or severe asthma) can have the illness become acute again as a result of a panic attack. Incidentally, this can also be caused by any other exertion.

Misconception: "I will faint"

If the symptoms worsen, especially dizziness, nausea, and clouded eyesight, those affected are usually convinced that they are losing their balance or even passing out. You try to stabilize yourself, hold on to something, or sit down so it doesn't get that far. Other people close to them believe them; Salespeople or helpful partners push them a chair or take them out into the fresh air. No one passes out during a panic attack.

Maybe someone says, "I remember fainting five years ago during a panic attack." But did he really pass out? Or almost passed out? Has he really lost consciousness? They may have passed out in the past for other reasons - during pregnancy, because of high blood pressure or due to anemia, after going to the sauna, or because they got up too quickly - but certainly not from the panic attack itself. These physical causes may not be present now, but because the person has passed out in the past, he fears that it may happen again. However, the fact is that it is impossible to pass out from a panic attack.

But there is also an exception to this rule. It affects people who are extremely anxious about anything having to do with medical treatment - hospitals, injections, the sight of blood, etc. During a panic attack, the body's energy levels usually increase - the heart beats faster, the breath becomes faster, we work up a sweat, etc., and blood pressure increases. However, fainting occurs when blood pressure is very low.

When some people see blood, their heartbeat slows down and their blood pressure drops rapidly. It is not only in the film that medical students who are in the operating room for the first-time faint at the sight of blood. In the real world, people may pass out when they see blood or splashes. It is possible to overcome this reaction over time, as some surgeons can tell you. In any case, this exception to the rule only applies to a few people. During a panic attack, the patient is so tense that he cannot pass out; the body just doesn't work that way. Those affected are too aroused and react too violently and are overstimulated to pass out.

Misconception: "I'm going to have a stroke"

Some people think a panic attack is a stroke, or they think a panic attack can get so bad that it causes a stroke. Others are more afraid of how they will fare after this supposed stroke - that they will become just "zombies" who can no longer take care of themselves, no longer talk, no longer eat themselves, and can no longer go to the toilet on their own. They often have elderly relatives who have had a stroke or are being cared for in a nursing home or hospital. Seeing them triggered the secret fear in these patients that one day they might feel the same way. It is a terrible thought for them to be dependent on others and in their fear, they imagine one day becoming severely disabled due to a panic attack. In reality, that never happens.

Misconception: "Something is wrong with my eyes"

What was bad for me were those horrible moments when my vision was suddenly blurry and my heart started beating like crazy.

When patients experience that they can no longer see clearly and that things seem to "float around", they tend to assume that something is wrong with their eyes or that they may even go blind.

It is difficult to imagine that the optic nerve, a very strong and thick nerve, could be damaged in any way by the fear response. Panic attacks cannot lead to permanent impairment of vision.

Chapter 7: The "my-body-wrecks-me" misconceptions

In the eyes of those suffering from panic attacks, our physical reactions no longer have the function of protecting and preserving us, but rather they see them as their enemy. During a panic attack, people fear that vital physical functions could suddenly stop and they would no longer be able to breathe, swallow, or move. If your attention is focused on this problem, it can create a vicious circle in two ways:

- You are trying to compensate; For example, if they feel that they are not getting enough air, they are trying hard to get more air into their lungs. However, this "compensation" makes them feel even more uncomfortable and hinders their natural (automatic) bodily functions.

- The fear of not being able to breathe, not swallowing, not being able to urinate, etc., only increases the feared unpleasant feelings. When a patient, for example, if he is afraid that he will no longer be able to swallow, his mouth will become completely dry and he will actually have difficulty swallowing - a self-fulfilling prophecy.

Misconception: "I will be paralyzed"

Some panic patients report symptoms of paralysis and they fear that they may become paralyzed in the long term. But that doesn't really happen; in this case, too, it is a matter of mere fear. They are based on brief subjective impressions that are misinterpreted and overrated in the mind of those affected. It often happens that "completely normal" people wake up in the morning with the feeling that they are paralyzed - they cannot move or breathe properly. This feeling is very uncomfortable, but as soon as you wake up properly, it will pass. However, if someone seriously begins to believe that they can remain paralyzed in the long term, then they simply get scared.

One of the standard tricks used by hypnotists is to ask their audience to fold their hands at the beginning of the performance. Then the hypnotist says with a tone of conviction that they would no longer be able to separate their hands from each other. What happens is this: Our knuckles hook into each other and offer some resistance when we try to detach our hands from each other. But we can try a little and then we succeed. However, some people say to themselves, when they begin to feel some resistance, "Yes, it's true. I cannot separate my hands from each other. I'm hypnotized. "All that comes next is autosuggestion. These are the people the hypnotist uses as guinea pigs - he knows that they will respond best to his suggestions. The idea of being paralyzed is similar. When we say to ourselves, "I'm paralyzed. I will never be able to move again", then it may be that our system overreacts and that we end up being really convinced that we will never get rid of these symptoms of paralysis. But - like almost all other strange symptoms that accompany panic - they pass and cannot cause permanent physical harm.

Misconception: "I will suffocate"

Certain changes often occur in the mouth and throat area during a panic attack that are a normal part of the body's fear response. The tension in the muscles in the neck area plays a major role in the feeling of suffocation. However, none of the changes mentioned are dangerous. Even if the patient has the impression that he is going to die, the muscles cannot possibly contract so much that he cannot breathe anymore and suffocates.

Sometimes patients try to compensate for fear of suffocation by eating slowly and swallowing very carefully. Some only eat soft, pulpy food and completely do without meat, nuts, and everything else that could get stuck in their throats.

Misconception: "I can't swallow"

During a panic attack, the victim's attention may be focused on the activity of the salivary glands, and thus the ability to swallow decreases. Very little saliva is produced as part of the fear response; this makes the mouth dry and makes it difficult to swallow. Some sufferers fear that their ability to swallow will be limited in the long term or that they will even lose it altogether. Some compensate by doing a test every few minutes - they swallow just to see if it can still be done. But this also has an unfavorable effect on the natural functions of the body and makes swallowing more painful and laborious. While this is not dangerous, it does make eating a rather unpleasant experience.

Misconception: "I can't breathe"

In a fearful situation, the body tries to take in more oxygen; therefore there are changes in our breathing rhythm - we breathe faster. Some people focus their attention on these changes and worry about their breathing. They may feel like they are not getting enough air, or they fear they are hyperventilating and harming themselves, or they may fear that their breathing will stop altogether. You may feel that you need to closely monitor your breathing and make sure you are breathing enough. All of this puts the completely normal and automatic bodily functions under voluntary control, and fear itself causes the breath to quicken. Breathing works best if you ignore it completely and leave it to its own rules. The body has amazing abilities to maintain the natural balance of oxygen and carbon dioxide in the blood.

Chapter 8. The "I-am-losing-my-mind" misconceptions

Misconception: "I'm going crazy"

Many people fear that they will lose control of themselves and go crazy during a panic attack. One patient put it this way:

I am then afraid that I will go crazy, that I will go nuts, that this will be the worst attack I have ever had. That it will be so bad that I will never recover from it and that I will fall into the blackest madness; you know, in a state of no going back. I then breathe very quickly and briefly. So then I breathe and the world collapses on top of me, everything falls on me, and that's the end, you know, there's just no way out. I just want to run away, then just get away, away, away.

When the feelings of panic intensify and when feelings of depersonalization, confusion, or loss of reality are added, those affected may think that this is a sign of the onset of mental illness, and of course, they will fight with all their might not to be overwhelmed by a condition which threatens to devour them once and for all.

In psychiatry, a distinction has been made for years between psychoses (real mental illnesses such as schizophrenia and manic depression) and neuroses, which are basically always symptoms of anxiety. The term "neurosis" is now out of date. It suggests a pathological disorder, and that is precisely not what a panic attack is. Besides, it has a negative connotation - think of "neurotics". Regardless of this, whatever expression we use to describe it, symptoms of anxiety are fundamentally different from mental illness. A patient suffering from anxiety is perfectly fine even if there are certain things in their life that they are not in control of as they would like. This has nothing to do with mental illness, which is always associated with significant changes in the person's thinking and behavior (including hallucinations, megalomania, paranoia, or the inability to think logically).

The many people who have once consciously allowed a panic attack without intervening in its natural course have found that, even if they temporarily lose accustomed control over their emotional life, they regain their emotional balance after a short time. After the attack, they find that they are completely unharmed and normal. The experience is similar to the emotional relief brought about by crying. The problem is not the alleged mental illness itself, but the fear of becoming insane or of losing control of one's own thinking and judgment.

Misconception: "I've lost control"

Common to all the misconceptions is the fear of losing control of certain bodily functions, of losing control of their own judgment, or of doing something terrible or embarrassing.

I'm going to do something stupid - slouch, scream, throw up, pee in my pants, or otherwise expose myself.

Some people are very concerned about how they will affect others during a panic attack and what they may think of them. Those affected think that the whole world should be aware of them because their feelings are so strong. But most people on the street or at work are so preoccupied with themselves and their own lives that they don't really pay attention to other people.

It's like having a pimple in your mouth. It feels huge, but when you look in the mirror you can see that it is only the size of the head of a pin. The fact that one's feelings are so strong does not mean that other people are just as aware of them or that we can be seen outwardly.

When people happen to see themselves in the mirror or in a shop window during a panic attack, they are amazed at how normal they look. They're not particularly interesting for the common man on the street, who rushes off to do their last shopping before closing time, or whose children are arguing about. Even if passers-by notice something, such as a person's face turning red, they tend to attribute it to the fact that the person concerned is apparently very warm or that they have high blood pressure - if they even notice.

Some people with panic attacks fear that if the panic gets worse, they may lose control of their physical functions and wet themselves or vomit. Others imagine losing control of their language and just talking gibberish. And still, others even imagine that it could get so bad for them that they run around like crazy, bump into people, knock things over and make themselves completely ridiculous. Or that they lose their minds and plunge into a nightmare from which there is no awakening - that they lose all control of themselves and become as helpless as a baby.

But those affected only imagine all this - in reality, something like this does not happen. It is important to distinguish between fear of loss of control and actual loss of control. One area of our nervous system is responsible for our feelings, and another for our actions. They work in completely different ways. We can hardly control our emotions, but we can control our actions despite all our fears.

VOMITING

Every time I came near a store and only thought about going in, I got very hot and terribly sick, and I was sure I couldn't go in there. I just couldn't risk vomiting in front of all the people.

Increased nausea that some people experience during a panic attack makes them fear that they will vomit, which would be terribly embarrassing for them.

Has the patient actually vomited during a panic attack in the past? Was there a special reason for this, for example, did you happen to have been infected with food at the same time? Most of the people who have this fear really don't vomit when they consciously allow a panic attack without interfering with its natural course. However, some patients report that they actually vomited during an attack. Sometimes they induce vomiting on purpose "to get it over with." Occasionally it is not about vomiting in the actual sense, but about the food coming back up again. In summary, it can be said that people whose main symptom is nausea during their panic attacks are very likely not to vomit; the basic possibility of doing this, however, exists, albeit on the margins.

GO TO THE TOILET

If I went anywhere, I was fine as long as I knew where the toilet was. But I got into real problems when I had to go somewhere I'd never been. Then I kept thinking about what would happen if I couldn't find a toilet in time, and I immediately had to go to the bathroom urgently.

Those affected imagine how embarrassing it would be if they were soaked in the presence of other people. For some patients, the strongest need to go to the toilet is the most noticeable symptom, and that leads to the fear: "What if I piss my pants now? That would be terrible!" In his imagination, the thought becomes almost a certainty.

Despite the strong urge to urinate and defecate, a panic attack does not cause those affected to wet or defecate. Even as small children we learned to keep our sphincters completely under our control, even in the deepest sleep. Why should we suddenly lose this ability when we are scared?

However, some persons with panic attacks may also be suffering from irritable bowel syndrome (IBS) which can cause urgency in them. Such urgency is not due to a panic attack.

DO DAMAGE TO OTHER

In the evenings when I got home from work I always did the usual things ... eat dinner, watch TV and all that, but sometimes this terrible fear of harming others would creep up in me, and then I would immediately get up and go out. I got in the car and drove around for hours until I felt the danger was over.

This man was afraid that if he had a panic attack at home, he would harm his wife. He was convinced that this would happen. Some patients fear that their feelings of panic could become so strong that they would completely lose control of themselves and injure or even kill their loved ones, strangers, or themselves. Or that they would run in front of a bus or jump out of a moving train. However, this is a misunderstanding; they believe that the fact that they cannot control their emotions means that they cannot control their actions either. But these are two very different things. You don't harm the people you love during a panic attack. Even if the feelings get mixed up those affected always keep control over their actions. If someone is afraid of hurting others, it means that is exactly what they don't want. Again, it is only a fear, not a real threat; in reality, those affected will not attack or hurt their loved ones.

A paper tiger?

In the last four chapters, we've covered many of the common fears people experience during a panic attack. It is perfectly normal and reasonable for people when confronted with sudden, unbearable feelings that they have never experienced before to have such fears and fears. Those having these symptoms and misconceptions are neither stupid nor crazy when they harbor such thoughts; however, these fears are plain and simply wrong. The fact is that panic attacks cannot harm you mentally or physically. A panic attack is like a snake that looks like a poisonous snake, but in reality, it is completely harmless - without teeth and without poison.

But how is it that during a panic attack one person fears one thing and another something completely different? The symptoms they both experience are more or less the same, but one may fear he has a heart attack and the other that he is insane.

Some patients have seen relatives die of a heart attack, or they have always secretly feared they would become insane. Such experiences can have a big influence on the thoughts that move people who suffer from panic attacks. Another reason may be that certain symptoms are very severe; so it is quite natural for someone whose heart is beating very quickly during an attack to fear that they have a heart condition. This then has nothing to do with any experiences he has made in the past.

Different people can have very different fears. What they all have in common, however, is that they fear some impending misfortune. We can even go so far as to say that they believe a lie or that their feelings have led them to believe they are in danger.

So is it the case that panic only happens in the head? No, not at all. The physical symptoms are really there. But the idea of what might happen during a panic attack is in the mind, in the imagination.

Chapter 9: What causes panic attacks?

The first panic attack a person experiences is often a complete surprise, like a bolt from the blue. There is no apparent reason for this to happen - the person did nothing unusual that day and was not exposed to any more stress than usual. It seems completely inexplicable why they suddenly panic. Even if panic attacks have later become an integral part of life, it often remains a mystery to those affected why panic attacks occur on some days and not on others.

The invisible connection

Even if a patient cannot see an obvious reason for the first panic attack, there is usually a connection to past events in that person's life. It is possible that the person concerned cannot see this connection - so this is "the invisible bond" - but it is there. The patient is probably unable to find an explanation for his panic attacks because he is looking in the wrong place. If we register very strong sensations in ourselves, then we look around to see if there is something in our immediate vicinity that triggers them. Is anything threatening me? Am I in danger? Do I have a dangerous disease? We may also wonder what we've been doing in the past hour or two. What did I eat Have I poisoned myself? Am I infected with a dangerous virus? Those affected rarely look back more than a day in their efforts to explain the panic attacks. That is why they often fail to see the real context - they are concerned with the wrong period.

Instead of looking for the causes in the last hour, day, or week, you should extend your search to the past one to nine months. You won't find anything at close range - you have to use the mind lens, so to speak, and focus your gaze on the medium distance.

What kind of stress were you under?

There are many studies that show that those affected went through a period of particular stress or traumatic experiences in the months before the first surprising panic attack, or that various stressful events came together. Here are some examples:

- death or illness of a partner, close relative, or friend;

- Operation or disability of partner;

- Marital problems: separation, quarrel, reconciliation after a period of separation, violent or very critical partner, imminent divorce;

- Children: the birth of a baby, miscarriage, stillbirth or abortion, illness or accident of a child, departure of an adult child from the parental home, responsibility for a young family;

- Family: Caring for an elderly parent, heavily controlling parent, or parents who meddle too much in their child's life;

- Leaving the parental home, finding a new job, starting studies, moving to a new apartment or a new area;

- Own physical health: surgery, illness, disability, menopause;

- Accidents: being involved in a car or other accident, seeing others get injured (hit by a car speeding by, etc.);

- Work: too much stress at work, deadline pressure, more responsibility, long working hours without breaks, boredom, bad working atmosphere, no promotion, too many problems at work, threatened or completed dismissal, retirement;

- Bankruptcy, money worries, problems with repaying loans;

- Use of legal or illegal drugs;

- Illness, also infectious disease.

Other, slightly less tangible, stressors that professionals have pointed out include:

- Separation experiences: leaving the parental home for the first time, separation through the death of the partner, separation from friends and familiar surroundings through moving;

- Feeling of being trapped, for example in an unhappy marriage, in a too-strenuous job, or living with relatives in an apartment;

- Loss of control over important areas of life, e.g., work or social life;

- Being controlled/suppressed by a parent or partner.

Pretty much any of the above stressors can set the ground up for panic attacks. Often one problem alone is not enough, but when two or three factors come together, the burden can become too great and our system "crashes".

RELAXATION

Another strange observation (which often puts a person on the wrong track) is that the first panic attacks sometimes occur during a period of calm and relaxation, during a long-awaited vacation, or after a period of particularly stressful stress has finally passed. It is as if a burden that has gradually built up and increased is suddenly taken away from a person and a panic attack attacks him instead.

A LITTLE TRIGGER

Aside from the background causes of panic, there is often a specific trigger, one last drop that brings the barrel to overflow. The "trigger" that set off the first attack is usually a relatively small, insignificant incident, the last drop which overflowed the barrel and eventually "blows the fuse."

What causes panic

Panic changes people - fear of further attacks draws their attention to the first signs of panic to which they are hypersensitive. The fear of these first symptoms sets a vicious circle in motion: the fear intensifies the symptoms, intensifies the fear, intensifies the symptoms, intensifies the fear, and so on and so on. Those affected are therefore afraid of another panic attack because they fear that they will be harmed -possibly having a heart attack, losing consciousness, or going crazy.

In order to avoid such unpleasant consequences, the patient begins to avoid certain places, situations, feelings, actions, thoughts, making appointments, and sometimes even falling asleep. These avoidance strategies cost those affected so much strength that their lifestyle gradually changes. And mostly they don't like the person they have become.

Two causes of panic

There is a whole world of invisible connections that patients are barely aware of. Most of the time, they don't realize that their first panic attack was triggered by stressful events in their life - worries or difficulties that began months before the first attack. In the days before the first attack, the victim's resistance may have been reduced; the panic attack may also have been prepared by a period of relaxation or triggered by a "trigger" event.

Usually, the patient does not associate the panic attack with the background causes, but explains it differently: He suspects a heart attack, a nervous breakdown, or a brain tumor.

The last link in the chain is then that the person concerned becomes afraid of the symptoms and it is precisely this that triggers panic reactions; this chain reaction then starts all over again, often over many years.

Thus there are two main reasons for panic attacks:

The original background cause *(s)* triggering *the first* panic attack;

After the first attack then the fear of further attacks.

Chapter 10. Address the background causes

There are two different causes of panic attacks. We must therefore offer therapeutic help for two different patient groups:

- for those who have failed to resolve the emotional problem that originally caused their panic attacks and who are also struggling with fear of further attacks. These people need help in two ways - they need to learn to recognize and cope with the original problem while gradually overcoming their "fear of fear";

- for those who have long since solved or overcome the underlying problem (e.g. the death of a parent), and now only have to struggle with the fear of further panic attacks. "Only" is of course not the right word here, because "fear of fear" can be so excruciating that it downright destroys the lives of those affected. Fear of feeling panic can bring it back to life again and again, even if the original reason no longer exists. In this second case, we do not need to concern ourselves with the background causes at all.

However, a person affected should not be misled into making assumptions like: "It's been five years since my husband died, so I have to be over it by now." Even when it is just pushed away, it's still there. It's buried under the surface like a mine that can detonate at any time. Time alone is not a measure of whether or not the problem has been overcome.

Can those affected identify which of the two groups they belong to?

If the person concerned has only recently suffered from panic attacks, one can assume that the causes are still effective. However, if the panic attacks started years ago, then over time the root causes may have faded into the background and become meaningless - they can, but they don't have to.

Is it possible to discover the causes yourself?

There are some difficulties that can prevent people from realizing the causes. Some of them are:

- The cause is not temporally related to the panic attack, so it does not seem to have anything to do with it.

- The cause doesn't seem important enough to trigger such a powerful attack.

- It is difficult for those affected to accept the fact that certain events in their life can trigger physical sensations.

- The causes are so painful that the patient has pushed them out of his consciousness.

- The patient is afraid of thinking about events that are emotionally upsetting.

- The patient believes that even if he calls it by its name, he cannot solve the underlying problem and that it is best to ignore it.

- The patient unconsciously does not allow the cause to come to light.

- There are several problems that interact and trigger panic reactions; however, each and every one of them seems so insignificant that the patient does not consider it as a possible cause.

A seven-point program for identifying the background causes of panic attacks

The following seven-point program is intended to help those affected to find out the possible causes of their panic attacks. You should work through this program point by point while being honest with yourself. You shouldn't consciously ignore anything that might be of any importance or pretend it's unimportant.

We all tend to suppress what upsets us and causes us anxiety. But it is best if we deal with painful events. When we see things at the edge of our consciousness then they usually do not disappear from our lives by themselves - they are still there and often draw attention to themselves in a form that is uncomfortable to us and whose meaning we cannot recognize. For example, by causing panic attacks.

Step One: Make a list of possible causes for your first panic attack

When did you have your first panic attack? Try to remember the date as precisely as possible and write it down.

Now consider the nine months leading up to this event in your mind. What happened in your life What changes have occurred, both positively and negatively? Write down everything you can remember, including what you may find insignificant.

First, write everything down and only later decide which events are possible causes. Make sure you also write down everything "forbidden" that you normally suppress because you do not want to think about it.

Step two: complete your list

Some important stressors from the areas of relationships, children, work, friends and relatives, health, accidents and accidents, finance, home and apartment, crime, and vocational training. Please add them to your list.

Third step: check how you feel about each point

Now read through your list one more time, point by point. Do you get sad, worried, or depressed about any of the events you wrote down, do you want to cry when you think about them? If any, underline them so that you can remember later that those things may be important.

Fourth step: talk to someone you trust

Share what you've found with someone who knows you well and whom you trust. Show or explain what you wrote down to him or her. Oftentimes, other people can see things that we ourselves overlook. It will likely help you see things in proper proportions.

Step five: revise your list

Now rewrite your list and order the events according to their importance. First, write down the event that seems most important to you, then the second most important, and so on. Take into account what your parents said (see step four), what you underlined (see step three), and also, what the "feelings in the stomach" tell you.

Step six: think about what you can do to defuse the problems

Next to each cause, write down what you could do about it to change the situation to solve the problem, or simply to feel better. Even if something has happened in the past there are still things you can do - ask a counselor, friend, or Imaam of a Mosque to talk to you, can cry or write your thoughts down, or you can pray about it.

Step seven: take action

Now start doing some of the things you wrote in point six.

Some changes can be dramatic, such as when you take on a new job. Of course, such an important decision requires you to think long and hard, and maybe seek advice from friends or your spouse, or just wait a while until you see more clearly. Sometimes even small changes can help a lot, for example, if you take a few days of vacation, organize your work better or cancel overtime. You can implement such changes as soon as possible.

Chapter 11: Process feelings and prevent panic attacks

Stress that is often unnoticed by the person affected and may have occurred months before the first panic attack can grow to such an extent that it triggers a panic attack. This is similar to the water that is dammed up behind a dam. The water rises inch by inch over the course of the months. The pressure is increasing all the time. At some point, it gets too big and the dam suddenly gives way. Huge masses of water pour through the broken dam and destroy the land beyond. Panic is like that too: sudden and destructive. Without the patient noticing it, the pressure built up over weeks and months. The panic attack seems to come suddenly, but it really does not. However, this dramatic comparison with the dam is a bit slow. Because it suggests that a sick person like the dam will be completely destroyed. This way is not correct. Man can get well.

The question now is why the person concerned did not notice that the pressure had increased. Why didn't he realize he was under stress? Why did he not notice the warning signals from his body: states of excitement, sleep disorders, feelings of anxiety, and lack of concentration? If these signs are interpreted correctly, a panic attack can be prevented.

There is another problem with the dam theory. Many people are confronted with very stressful situations in their lives - the death of a loved one, termination, or illness. If such stress can trigger panic attacks why doesn't everyone who leads a stressful life have panic attacks?

There are the following aspects:

- The person concerned tries to suppress or repress every emotion.

- He is silent about his feelings and does not share them with others.

- He does not express his feelings in words or deeds.

- He concentrates on the physical symptoms and not on the feeling itself. For example, he perceives clenched teeth, a hot face, sweating, tremors, and excitement, but not the feeling of anger that is hidden behind them.

- He lacks the connection between event and emotion. This is how he feels rejected if a friend ignores him, but fails to relate this feeling of rejection to the behavior of the friend.

Could these difficulties in processing emotions be related to panic? Is it possible that a person who cries or scolds in the face of a difficult or stressful life situation or speaks openly about it with friends or relatives can process and calm down his complex feelings correctly? This prevents the stress from building up to the point where the dam breaks. But what about people who suffer a severe loss or have a painful experience in their life, keep it to themselves, do not talk to others about it, or express their feelings in tears or anger? This is the moment when the water behind the dam begins to rise.

Panic patients control their emotions to a much greater extent than non-sick subjects. The panic patients not only control disturbing, anxious, or worried feelings, which might seem logical to them but also control anger and sadness to an exaggerated degree. Compared to the others who don't suffer from panic attacks, the panic attack patients also had greater difficulty identifying feelings and relating emotions to the events that caused them. Rather, they agreed with the following statements:

- I suppress my emotions.

- I suppress my feelings.

- I'm silent about my feelings.

- I find it difficult to name my emotions.

When panic sufferers fail to properly process difficult emotional events, this opens up opportunities to help them. If we develop better strategies for processing emotions, it may be possible to prevent the onset of panic or, if it has already started, aid recovery. An exception to the dam theory is panic caused by drug use. In addition to drug use, stress may have built up here, but in some cases, the drug is enough to trigger the first panic attack.

How to better process feelings

The system a person uses to process emotions is a bit like our immune system. It has to be functional to protect us from the pressures and stresses of life. We strengthen our immune system through good nutrition, adequate sleep, and rest - but how can we ensure that our "emotional immune system" is working properly?

The right attitude

First of all, it is important to develop the right attitude towards emotions. In our childhood and adolescence, we usually adopt unspoken attitudes towards feelings: whether it is right to have feelings, how to express them, what is "normal" and what is "abnormal". These attitudes or "rules" may come from our culture, from the environment in which we grew up, or from our family.

In some families, an unspoken rule is that feelings should be tightly controlled and that showing feelings is wrong or a sign of weakness. In other families, the rule is that feelings are okay, but that having negative feelings is somehow unhealthy. Some families do not accept or discuss feelings at all. Whatever your background - and there are so many different "rules" - we all have unspoken attitudes towards feelings.

But what is a healthy attitude now?

- Having feelings is normal and healthy.

- Having both positive and negative feelings are normal and healthy.

- Experiencing feelings is usually not subject to conscious control. Rational thinking can be controlled and directed in certain directions, but feelings don't work that way. We cannot expect them to "obey" us.

- Feelings are part of being human. If there were only positive feelings, we would not be able to respond appropriately to the ups and downs of life. We'd have a frozen smile on our face and we'd be happy whether we'd won the lottery or our best friend died. Being able to experience positive feelings means that negative feelings are also possible.

- Feelings can't harm us. They are a part of a normal, healthy body.

- Feelings are not primitive, nor are they inferior to reason or logic. The psychologist Richard S. Lazarus put it this way: "We have a mind and it contains both thoughts and feelings. Passion and reason come together here. There is nothing more human than reason and feeling. What we need is the right balance."

- Feeling emotions is not the same as acting emotionally. Feeling anger is not the same as reacting angry, such as yelling at, berating, or beating someone. In some situations, emotional actions are right, but not in others. It is not particularly harmful to control our actions, but it is harmful to control our emotional state.

Allowing emotional experiences

Basically, it is best not to suppress or control emotions, or to switch off or distance yourself from your emotions. It is understandable, however, that people with constant uncomfortable panic would wish they could keep their feelings under control. This however clogs the entire emotional life. The difficulty with panic patients is that they perceive every feeling as a danger. In their eyes, the whole world seems dangerous. Something else is necessary for them: They have to learn not to assess every feeling, every excitement, and every emotion as threatening. Feelings may not be pleasant, but they are not dangerous.

Pearls of wisdom

Every emotion contains important information; it is a "pearl of wisdom". That sounds pretty strange, especially when you think of constant panic feelings. But in general, it is the case that our feelings contain information about the world around us, about our relationships with other people, and about our own well-being.

To get the most out of the "pearls of wisdom" contained in your emotions, there are three simple steps:

Step 1: Be aware of your feelings

The first step is that you try to sense your emotions. You may ask yourself, "How do I feel at this moment?", or: "How do I feel about my life at the moment?" What physical symptoms and feelings do you perceive? Do not put pressure on yourself to judge or understand your feelings. For now, stick to sensing these feelings and focusing on them. Just like an appraiser does an appraisal of a home, you are an emotional appraiser. The appraiser checks the whole house and takes in the most important facts, but he is not emotionally attached to the house. He has a certain distance and tries to see the house objectively. Therefore, in the first step, you should only observe your feelings and become aware of their characteristics: How intense are they, where in the body are they located, how big are they and what are their characteristics? You should make these observations without getting drawn into the feeling.

Step 2: Name your feelings

The second step is to name the feeling. Is it anger or frustration that you can't talk, or frustration that your brother keeps interrupting you when you want to say something important? Each label is measured again on the feeling to see how well it fits. By applying the term to the feeling, you can formulate this term more and more precisely. Just being able to name feelings correctly can be very liberating. So this is the "labeling", the "naming".

Step 3: Connect Feelings to Causes

The third step follows automatically when you have learned to name your feelings. When a feeling is properly named it should be possible to relate it to the event that caused the feeling. This event could be someone continually criticizing, betraying, or controlling you, or it could be realizing how unhappy you are at your job. The feeling provides the key to the cause.

For panic sufferers, it may be better not to start these three steps with feelings of fear or panic, because it is difficult to be objective about something that overwhelms you. Perhaps you can start by focusing on situations that make you angry or sad. You should proceed as described above: Objectively perceive feelings, name them and finally connect them to the causes.

Shared pain is half of the pain

Some patients succeed in naming emotions, but not others. Another useful way to help process emotions is to talk to someone. Talking to a friend, relative, or counselor you trust can be hugely helpful in two ways: first, it enables you to get your feelings out of your mind, and second, it helps you see things in another light. The other person can suggest thoughts or paths that you have not yet considered yourself.

Troubleshooting

Once you understand what is causing your emotional problem, there is an opportunity to resolve it.

Sleep and maybe even dream

The processing of emotions happens mostly unconsciously and quite naturally. This all works pretty well when left to its own devices. People have known about the healing power of sleep for many years.

Words, words, words

It can be part of the panic illness that you try over and over again, like on a treadmill, to understand or analyze what is happening. In a way, that can make a person think too much. One direction in Chinese philosophy is that a person's life can be unbalanced if he thinks too much, is too cerebral, or is too analytical. It is important that you fill your time with activities that affect other areas of the brain, such as a visit to the park, a visit to an art gallery, or a trip to the countryside - preferably things that have nothing to do with words.

A happy heart is a good medicine

It seems obvious, but there is even a solid line of research out there trying to show that processing negative experiences is easier when you do enjoyable things, focus on fun and humor, and allow yourself a good time. That doesn't mean you should be walking around and laughing artificially - that would be a big hoax. It is important to be honest with your feelings. The best way to approach this is to get involved in activities that usually make you laugh or enjoy yourself. Do happy things and leave your feelings to their own devices.

All of these considerations and suggestions can help us deal with, understand, and relate to the negative experiences that cause our suffering. This is better than hiding from them, denying them, or repressing them.

It is pointless to not want to think about something. The more you fight the thoughts, the worse they become!

Is there an antidote to thoughts?

There are two different antidotes. They depend on which thought processes are typical for the person concerned.

If you are afraid of certain thoughts - such as hurting yourself or others - and you are spending time and energy trying to suppress or get rid of those thoughts, then the antidote is to face the cause of your fear. Running away does not work. You should expose yourself with the help of your doctor or therapist to confront your fears.

Some obsessive thoughts, such as doubting what you did or didn't do, or doubts about your state of mind, can take many hours to try to think yourself out of the depths. You want to make sure you are normal, or you want to try to undo the past. You want to get the feeling that everything is fine again. For example, the obsessive thought "I'm going out of my mind" worries and deeply upsets the person concerned. Therefore, he tries to convince himself that his mind is fine. The problem is that this can take hours and that thoughts turn in circles over and over again. Well-trodden thought paths can be embarked on anew every day. The state of restlessness and the hoped-for feeling of confirmation (to be normal) or reassurance drive the person concerned to rethink the whole thing over and over again.

Sometimes the person concerned gets a certain confirmation, a kind of haven or oasis, for a while, but then the same doubt returns and everything starts all over again.

Usually, his thinking gets stuck somewhere in the middle before he gets the satisfying feeling of conclusive evidence. If this is the pattern, then the antidote is to step off the beaten path. The point is to stop looking for evidence and to live with the feeling of worry, uncertainty, or doubt until it goes away on its own - which is sure to happen. If the person becomes concerned and does not go through the usual rituals to reverse what has happened, the concern will subside after a week or two.

Chapter 12: Everything depends on your attitude!

The success of your therapy depends crucially on your inner attitude. You must know,

- how to cope with good and bad days,

- how to deal with setbacks,

There will always be setbacks. Setbacks are completely normal. Therapy does not fail because there are setbacks, but only if the person concerned reacts incorrectly to setbacks. Let us now look at a few different attitudes that you, the person affected, might have.

Good and bad days

"Bad days" when a patient is suffering from anxiety and feelings of depression can be very daunting. It is quite normal for anxiety and panic sufferers to have good days and bad days. They experience one or more days when they feel relatively normal. Then, for no apparent reason, the terrible symptoms reappear. Sometimes this nasty haunt lasts longer than a few days - maybe a whole week.

Sometimes people do not realize why they are having a bad day and that can make them very worried. Sometimes bad days are the result of changes, stress, or fatigue, sometimes physical illness such as the flu, sometimes premenstrual tension, and sometimes they are simply due to the sufferer no longer having the right attitude towards their fears and falling back into old habits is that make his situation worse. And sometimes there just doesn't seem to be any reason for a bad day at all.

Bad days are normal

All people have good and bad days; however, most do not attach particular importance to bad days. They may not be particularly comfortable, but they don't care too much. For panic patients, however, a bad day has a completely different meaning. They seem to know as soon as they wake up that they are going to have a bad day; they are under tension all day and fear having a panic attack. They regret it and get upset when they've been doing just fine for a while and then another darned day comes - like one "Friend" who always stands in front of the door at the most inopportune moment and wants to have a chat. It is very important that those affected learn to accept good and bad days as something completely normal - that they are not too euphoric about good days and not too depressed about bad ones.

Therapy with your doctor or psychologist is like riding a bike for the first time. It takes a while to get it right. If someone says, "It won't work - I'll never learn this" the first time they fall, they are probably giving up and really not learning. You have to be aware that setbacks are part of the learning process, dust off your clothes, and rise again.

Before embarking on this part of therapy, you should firmly anchor the thought that setbacks are completely normal and to be reckoned with, and how to deal with them if you experience them.

Over time, the successes become noticeable

When a person begins to feel better, they notice the bad days more. Let's say someone has a panic attack every other day at the start of therapy. His condition is getting better and he has not had a panic attack for five days. He feels that life is worth living again and begins to hope that this time he will really make it. Then, on the sixth day, he has another attack. The old misery is coming back and you can hardly blame him for what he thinks, "It was all just imagination. I will never change." This reaction, however, is indicative of the person's underlying misconception. We could call it the "overnight healing" attitude - the idea that our problem should go away completely from one day to the next. That's not the case. In the course of therapy, however, we will experience more and more good days and fewer and fewer bad ones.

Be a long-distance runner

The most important thing is that you learn to think in the long run. Your life can change. So on a bad day, here's what you should do:

- realize that this is only a temporary setback;

- do not give up hope; think about the progress you've made and that there will be good days again;

- Keep in mind that if you continue with what has helped you, you will be successful again.

The three buts

There are three fairly common reasons that people refuse therapy:

But I've had this for too long

If someone has had panic attacks for many years, then such a reaction is very understandable. But it doesn't matter if someone has had this problem for two months or twenty years - it can be fixed! A standard work on agoraphobia deals with the question of whether there are certain factors that allow conclusions to be drawn as to which patients will make progress in the course of therapy and which will not. The authors come to the conclusion that: "The therapist should not be discouraged when patients are very anxious or slightly depressed or if they have fairly pronounced and long-lasting phobias. Surprising results can also be achieved with severely disabled or disadvantaged patients."

When people have had anxiety disorders for so long they give up hope. If they feel better for a day, they first say to themselves, "It's gone!", But then "it" comes back, over and over again, until they give up all hope of a cure. Some people are so familiar with the fear that they feel really weird when they get better. It's like suddenly missing a trusted comrade, and they almost seem to be looking around for something to worry about. No one can promise a complete cure with 100% certainty, but with the help of information, understanding, and the right approach, the chances of overcoming panic disorders are very good.

But these feelings paralyze me so much

A typical hallmark of panic attacks is that the feelings they are experiencing are so strong and that they seem to increase dramatically during the course of an attack. Symptoms can be severe enough to make it difficult for them to concentrate or do the simplest of everyday tasks. As far as therapy is concerned, however, it makes little difference how severe or how numerous the symptoms are or how often panic attacks occur. The same principles are used throughout and the same good results are achieved.

But I've already tried that

This is also what patients sometimes say when this part of the therapy is explained to them. Yes, they've tried it, but they've tried a little of this and a little of this. A magazine article recommended this and a friend recommended this. Once they tried a relaxation tape, then they did it for a while. It's like being tossed back and forth in waves - a little bit this way and then a little bit that way.

What matters is:

- Determination: You have to keep going, day after day, week after week. There will be setbacks, there will be defeats. What must not be present are regret and despair. There should just be an unwavering advance.

- The right approach: Of course, there is no point in someone going on and on, but in the wrong direction; he never gets where he wanted to. He has to be sure that the direction is right and that the method is right for him - and then stick with it.

Chapter 13: The individual elements of the fear response

Whether panic attacks were originally caused by someone being trapped in an unhappy marriage, losing a child, moving out of home, or being under pressure for any other reason, fear kicks in as soon as someone experiences their first panic attack in his life.

When fear knocks on the door

Those affected are afraid of further panic attacks and fear of their possible causes and consequences. They don't understand what is happening to them.

In this chapter, the fear reaction is described in more detail. This will help those affected to better understand their own fear and to find a way out of the "vicious circle of fear". Perhaps those affected do not even refer to their reaction to panic attacks as fear. They may call them "discomfort" or "concern," or they may have succeeded so well in avoiding further panic attacks that they cannot detect fear in themselves.

The fear reaction in slow motion

The fear response happens so quickly that it is not easy to see what is happening in detail.

Some video devices have a button on their remote control that can be used to slow down a movie. You can let a movie go so slowly that you can see it and be able to look at it picture by picture and see details that are impossible to see when watching the film at a normal pace. Suppose we could similarly slow down the fear response. What would we find out?

FIRST PICTURE

We would see that the very first element of the fear response has nothing to do with feeling "fear". At first, it is only about "taking notice".

In the technical language of psychologists, this part of the fear reaction is called the assessment of a situation as dangerous situation. In other words, before someone feels fear, they have to recognize that there is an impending danger. That is what is meant by assessing the situation.

This assessment can be a very simple sensory perception, for example when we see a snake or flames flickering around us.

These "simple" dangers seem to trigger a natural, automatic response in both humans and animals. Another "automatic" fear trigger is noise. Generals have always known this and ordered their troops to hoot and scream loudly when attacking the enemy.

Let's take another example: imagine we're walking down a dark street in the city center late at night. At the end of it, we suddenly see the outlines of two men. It seems that they are waiting for us at the end of the street.

Our assessment here implies a fairly high level of mental activity. It is based on the knowledge that in cities at night under cover of darkness when there are few people crimes are often committed. And that a person standing at the end of a passage cuts our way. And that two male figures who cut our way in such a place mean danger. Even if this assessment is made in an instant, it is based on thought, knowledge, and experience.

In other words: before our body perceives fear, we must first have recognized a dangerous situation. This recognition can be a simple perception of naturally dangerous objects or the result of our deliberations and experiences with regard to what is dangerous for us.

SECOND PICTURE

The next picture of the slow-motion shot concerns the physical sensations - all the symptoms: sweating, palpitations, shortness of breath, muscle tension, tremors, choking, hot flashes, chest pain, dizziness, lightheadedness, etc. As this chapter explains, the fear reaction, which is essentially the same for all people, enables us to react quickly and effectively to a dangerous situation. As soon as a situation is assessed as dangerous (first picture), the fear reaction and the associated symptoms automatically occur.

THIRD PICTURE

The third element of the fear response concerns the way we behave. The strong feelings of fear cause us to take action. The usual options are escape, fight, or freeze.

A twelve-year-old boy was attacked by a grizzly bear in the Rocky Mountains. He described how the bear attacked him with his front paws and struck his claws in him; then he dropped to the ground as if lifeless and pretended to be dead. A few days earlier he had heard a couple of trappers say that bears will let go of a person if they think they are dead. He lay very still and the bear actually trotted away. The boy felt the typical feelings of fear (second picture) that would normally have caused him to flee, but his knowledge of bears enabled him to overcome this impulse and lie very still. He was able to control his reaction to feelings of fear.

We have now let our »film« run extremely slowly in order to be able to clearly recognize the individual elements of the fear reaction.

In reality, the fear response is so rapid that it seems as if various steps are being taken at the same time.

What we think makes the difference

An interesting and important fact is that our feelings of fear are triggered by believing that we are in danger. If we do not think that we are in a dangerous situation, then our body does not react with fear. On the other hand, if we believe we are in danger when it is not, then our body reacts just as if it were actually in danger. It all depends on our assessment of the situation here.

Different assessment options:

- assess a dangerous situation as dangerous,

- assess a dangerous situation as harmless,

- assess a non-dangerous situation as dangerous.

What most people consider dangerous is outside of themselves - they fear that something "out there" could harm or kill them. What panic patients perceive as threatening lies within themselves - it is their own feelings and sensory perceptions. When certain bodily sensations signal danger, the person concerned is constantly on the lookout for them and inwardly adjusting their antennae to detect signs of imminent danger. And, of course, one often experiences such changes in physical well-being over the course of a day. This means that panic patients are signaled danger several times a day and feel feelings of fear. As a result, they live in the hell of their own fears every day.

Misunderstood danger

Panic patients definitely belong to the third category - they interpret situations as dangerous when in reality they are not dangerous. In other words, they react exactly as another person would react if they were threatened by a knife. Your emotional response is perfectly fine. The only wrong thing is that they mistakenly assume they are in danger when in truth there is none.

Please stop for a moment and understand what this means. It means that panic sufferers are completely normal people. Your mind works perfectly normally. Your emotional response to danger is just as it should be. You are neither insane nor unstable. They are perfectly normal people who simply made a mistake. They believe that a panic attack that takes its natural course will harm them. Anyone else who thought so would react just like her.

So the problem is a misjudgment, and the solution is to discover that panic attacks are, in fact, not dangerous.

Where should the therapy start?

At which element of the fear response should therapy begin? If we tried to change the feelings of fear (second picture) it could harm the person; the next time he is faced with danger, he may not be able to respond appropriately to it. It would be possible to change the behavior resulting from the feelings of fear (third picture), as did the boy who was attacked by a grizzly bear. But even if they were able to change their behavior, they would still feel unpleasant feelings of fear. The therapy of cognitive disability starts with the erroneous assessment that panic attacks are dangerous (first picture). When people know that panic attacks are safe, they will no longer feel anxious.

Chapter 14: Take the sting out of fear

How can a person realize that panic attacks, while uncomfortable, are by no means dangerous? By asking others who have had panic attacks? By talking to a friend about it? By listening to a therapist or an expert speaking on a television or radio show? Sometimes panic sufferers hear from other people that panic is safe and then pay lip service, but at the bottom of their hearts, they are not convinced of it.

How can one get at the inner conviction of a person?

What has to change is the deep inner conviction of those affected. They deeply believe that if they let a panic attack take its natural course, something terrible would happen.

You may not be able to say exactly what that something could be, but it is definitely something very bad. They could potentially die, go insane, or lose control of themselves. Yes, it would be possible, and it would be very, very uncomfortable - you cannot get rid of this inner certainty.

How can you get hold of these deeply rooted beliefs? It's hard to force yourself to change your mind, no matter how convincing the arguments may sound. Inner convictions are not so easy to explain away. The best way to find out what is really happening is through personal experience; the affected have to discover the truth for themselves. They have to embark on an experiment to see whether what they believe is true or not.

The personal experiment

When scientists make an experiment, it is always designed to test their theory; the result will either confirm or refute their theory. If you were to say: "I already know the answer; we don't need to check it," then others would say, "Prove it!" If they were to do an experiment that could only prove that their theory is correct, that would not be a real test. A scientific experiment is more like tossing a coin that reveals a head or an eagle if it stays where it is - it has to either confirm or refute the theory at hand.

And what is the "personal experiment" about? It is intended to prove or disprove something that is of great importance to a person's daily life. People suffering from panic attacks can do an experiment to find out what will happen to them if they allow a panic attack to follow its natural course.

Enter unknown land

At this point, those affected may say: "But I've been through this a thousand times. I know exactly what is happening." However, they are essentially like scientists who have never really tested their theory. Here are a few factors that can prevent the crucial experiment:

- You remember your first bad panic attacks that seem carved into your memory and are completely fixated on them. So it is difficult for them to face the present and to examine impartially what would happen today.

- Your fear of what might happen is so great that you assume it will happen. However, this is only a guess, not a proven fact.

- Because the feelings that accompany a panic attack are so uncomfortable, they have focused entirely on their feelings and not paid any attention to what is actually happening.

- You have long avoided certain places, situations, actions, and feelings or taken "safety measures" to avoid panic attacks from the outset. So they never had to ask themselves the crucial question of what would happen without all of these precautionary measures.

- Their "lifesavers", through which they defuse their panic attacks (deep breathing, relaxation, alcohol, etc.), ensure that the attacks never reach their natural climax. So you never know what would happen if a panic attack just took its course.

In the following, a person affected reports that she carefully planned her everyday life in all details in order to avoid anything that could have triggered a panic attack:

I just know; that I've been planning everything this way for years; this planning has become an integral part of my life. I am a real expert at it. I can think incredibly quickly and keep making up white lies and plausible excuses. Nobody who was in any way involved in my planning; ever suspected this. But it all takes so much strength that would be better used for other things. The only problem is, if I just let things take their course, I'll be entering a completely unknown land.

In order to find out what is really happening, the person concerned has to enter this "unknown land" and that takes a lot of determination, courage, and a little planning.

Conduct a personal experiment

Here are the steps a person affected can take to find out what really happens during a panic attack.

The first thing he has to ask himself is, "If I had a panic attack and didn't try to control it, stop it, or in any way escape it, what could happen? What am I afraid of?"

Some people find it difficult to answer this. You may say that they are not afraid that anything special will happen. When patients are asked, "What would happen if you went out of business if you had a panic attack?" They sometimes say, "But I would never let it get that far." In other words, they dispose about such a sophisticated system of avoidance strategies that they no longer have to think about what might happen. Sufferers should drop all of these strategies and say what the worst would be that could happen.

After putting into words what they are afraid of, they should conduct a series of personal experiments to see if this is really happening.

Such an experiment would include the following points:

1) Refrain from avoidance strategies and consciously bring yourself into a panic-inducing situation

This can mean, for example:

- to consciously go to certain places;

- intentionally putting yourself in certain situations;

- to allow certain feelings;

- to consciously deal with certain upcoming events;

- to perform certain acts that induce fear;

- Allowing thoughts of panic;

- no longer trying to forego sleep.

2) Do not take any action that is appropriate to prevent a panic attack

3) After the start of a panic attack, do nothing> that weakens its course (do without "lifesavers")

In other words, patients must consciously expose themselves to a panic attack without intervening in its course. Only after following steps 1, 2, and 3 can you really know what is happening during a panic attack. If they put the test to the test and find that they won't die, pass out, lose control, and so on, then their panic will gradually diminish. Of course, panic patients find such experiments very threatening. In their opinion, they are being asked to put their life or health at risk.

Chapter 15: Prepare your personal test series

Let us now work out a detailed set of personal experiments for you that will help you learn to understand and overcome your fears from the ground up. You can take a few steps in consultation with your doctor to find out what is really happening during a panic attack:

- Make a list of the situations that are particularly difficult for you or that can cause panic. This list could look something like this:

  1) Crowds, especially in large department stores

  2) standing in line

  3) Being in a store without seeing the exit

  4) Sitting at home in the evening and relaxing

  5) climb stairs

- Now write down the "safety measures" that you take in the relevant situations to avoid a panic attack. For example:

1) Crowds

I take a sedative before leaving the house.
I'm taking a friend with me.
I avoid large department stores and only go to small shops.
I only shop on weekdays when there are fewer people around.
I only go shopping spontaneously (when I'm feeling good). I only socialize on "good days".

2) stand in line

I don't go to supermarkets.
I always queue for the shortest line.
I only buy a few things at a time.

3) Being in a business:

I avoid businesses in which I could get "trapped".

I always stay close to the exit.

I make sure that I can always see the exit. I make sure that I can always see my friend/partner.

4) Sitting relaxed at home in the evening

I always do something.

I keep doing things in my mind to distract myself.

I take care not to watch TV for too long.

I always stay tense inside.

I don't watch anything that upsets me - no scenes of violence and no programs about mental disorders.

5) Climbing stairs

I'm not doing anything that requires me to exert a lot of effort in a short period of time.

I sneak up the stairs.

I make sure that I don't have to go up too often.

- Make a list of your "life savers"; write down everything you do to lessen or stop a panic attack. This could include, for example:

I take a deep breath.

I try to relax.

I tell myself, "Nothing will happen. It's all right."

I take a pill.

I look around for a chair and sit down.

I lie down on the bed.

I look around for a wall and lean against it.

I'm running somewhere.

I slap myself.

I shake my head violently.

I'll call the doctor or a good friend.

I drink water.

I try to distract myself by reading or doing mental arithmetic.

As a data subject, you should do the following:

- consciously put oneself into feared situations (e.g., crowds of people),

- while doing this on safety measures (such as tranquilizers)

- and do without "lifesavers" (for example deep breaths).

It is very advisable to write down in writing (for example in the form of a diary) what you have achieved and how you felt.

Every time you try something new, you can rate the feelings that accompany it

Step by step

Some people, once they understand what it is about, want to "take the bull by the horns" and immediately face the situation that frightens them most. Others are more cautious and may need a friend or relative to help them in the beginning. If so, then that person should also read this book to make sure they understand what panic attacks are and what is important to treat them. In most cases, the person will have to conduct a number of personal experiments.

First of all, the person affected might want to try something that doesn't seem too difficult - for example, to sit relaxed at home in the evening. As a first experiment, he (she) may decide to watch TV for an hour without distracting himself, jumping up in between, and doing other things. At this point, he (she) may want to watch a "safe" program (no violence and nothing about mental illness). In further experiments, he (she) may then consciously choose a more difficult program or simply switch on the television at random without knowing what is being broadcast.

What will those affected find out after their first experiment?

Did you panic? If so, could they let these feelings go and bear them until they stopped on their own? What did you learn? What else needs to be verified through further experiments?

Perhaps, if the first experiment went well, they might mistake the first experiment and just repeat it again to see if the same thing happens again. After this second experiment, you may have gained more confidence and will do a slightly riskier experiment next.

After this experiment, you may have the impression that you can handle the panic that occurs at home. However, you are not sure if they could do just as well "outside". You still need many "mini-experiments" to confirm the results of the first experiments. But the next important experiments should take place "outside". Perhaps the next step is to try going to a supermarket, and then later, waiting in line at a supermarket. Later still, you may try to do the same thing on a "bad" day. In the course of the series of experiments, you will probably become aware to what extent you have so far protected yourself from feelings of panic, and if all goes well, you gradually cease your efforts to suppress and control panic. Most of the time it takes a whole series of personal experiments to come to terms with the many different aspects of their fears.

Four basic rules for a meaningful series of experiments

The main goal of the experiments is to get a panic attack

If those affected have carried out the experiments without ever having a panic attack - what have they learned from them? You may have learned something useful - that panic attacks are less common than you thought - and that can be very encouraging. However, it harbors a secret danger. Imperceptibly and almost automatically, they lose sight of the actual goal of the therapy, and when they finally do have a panic attack, it throws them completely off track and takes their courage away. But the only thing that went wrong was that, in their eyes, success equated to "don't get scared," while real success is getting through a panic attack. If someone doesn't experience a single panic attack in the course of their therapy, then they think that everything will go well in the future too. However, the likelihood is high that they will one day have a panic attack or "mini-panic attack" and then cannot cope with it. Experiencing panic yourself is the best immunization for the future.

Facing what one fears most in the eye will be uncomfortable, maybe even utterly terrifying

Patients will be very uncomfortable and terrified and it will take a great deal of courage. If they give up their usual security measures and face fear in the face of the monster, they are often even worse off than before; the new behavior saps their strength, and they are agitated and exhausted. But after this stressful time they will - if they are able to deal with their fears to confront the worst fear - discover that behind their fear there is no real danger, and as a result, their condition will gradually improve. One could call this experience "unpleasant but not dangerous."

You have to give yourself enough time for each experiment

Watching TV for a few minutes or walking into a crowd usually won't help much. There is not much they can learn from it. You have to take your time doing the experiment until you find out what you wanted to find out. You should give yourself around forty-five minutes for each experiment. If you set a certain period of time in advance, then this fact alone can be enough to trigger a feeling of being fixed and, as a result, a panic attack. If, on the other hand, you allow yourself the freedom to evade an unpleasant situation at any time, then this can mean that a panic attack never occurs. It is therefore a good idea to commit to a certain period of time. It is amazing, how something frightening can lose its horror if you only confront it long enough. Sometimes a particular fear can lose its power without the person being able to tell when exactly it happened. Some situations or activities that were previously very fearful become plain and simply boring after a while.

Sufferers should never try to escape from a situation when they feel intense or growing fear - it only makes things worse. You should try not to leave a situation until the fear has peaked or if it wasn't very strong in the first place.

Choose the next personal experiment

After each experiment, the person concerned should ask: "What else do I have to do to convince myself that panic is safe and does not pose a threat to me?" Or: "What are my deepest fears?" The answers can be used as pointers and guidelines for further experiments.

In most cases, those affected will first carry out their personal experiments on "good" days. Then what do they learn? They learn that they can get by on "good" days, but they still feel uncomfortable at the thought of doing certain things on "bad" days. Perhaps something terrible would happen on a day like this when anxiety and depression are so close. This question gives an important clue as to what the next experiment should be - deliberately attempting the same on a "bad" day! If those concerned discover that panic is safe even then, then that takes much of the power of the "bad" days; they are also becoming rarer.

The speed at which the individuals concerned tackle their experiments will vary from person to person. Everyone should do it the way they like. The only important thing is that with each experiment, people learn something new about panic.

Chapter 16: Possibilities, difficulties, and limits

Why would anyone take on all the pain and fear that these personal experiments bring? Patients have to do what they are most afraid of, and that can be excruciating at times. Is it even worth it?

What is all this for?

The results that are usually achieved by the therapy described:

- Panic attacks occur less often.

- The panic attacks are no longer that severe.

- Even if there are occasional panic attacks, those affected find them uncomfortable, but no longer frightening.

- Those affected feel more relaxed; they no longer need to fight panic attacks.

- The ingenious system of avoidance strategies, safety measures, and "life savers" is gradually beginning to dissolve.

- The general mood of those affected improves; they become more courageous and less prone to depression and fear.

- You are no longer dependent on tranquilizers or mood enhancers.

- You will be able to cope better with your life and develop personally.

- Those affected experience an inner liberation that has a positive effect on their social contacts, their professional life, and their leisure activities.

And what if I don't have the strength to do such personal experiments?

That is entirely up to the individual to decide. Everyone is different, and what is good for one does not necessarily have to be good for another. For many people it is enough if they are theoretically well informed about panic attacks; others, on the other hand, have to make all the experiences themselves.

A patient may be simply too scared to engage in any experiment, or they may not be convinced that it is necessary. In such a case, it may be better not to use it. Some give it a try and then have to give up - there is no way they should think they have failed.

In these experiments, those affected often need a lot of support from close relatives.

Expert guidance and support from a therapist are often required. In such cases, a self-help book is simply not enough. What should these people do? You will likely need the personal attention and knowledgeable help of a clinical psychologist trained in cognitive behavioral therapy, and possibly drug treatment as well.

Those affected should first seek the advice of their family doctor and, if necessary, ask him to refer them to a psychotherapist.

The therapist will then give the patient the opportunity in an initial consultation to express himself in detail about his problem. At this point, he can often see why the person in question is unsuccessful with the approach described in this book, and offer his own suggestions for solutions. Of course, every therapist has his own method, and not all of them work with the same approach. But there are many advantages to being able to speak from person to person, especially if the other person is familiar with the problem.

There are also a number of self-help groups for anxiety and panic patients, most of which are run by those affected themselves. They are often of great help as they make individuals feel like they are not alone with their problems and are receiving help and support.

The person concerned can best judge whether he (or she) wants to do the suggested exercises or not. If not, then there is absolutely no reason to be ashamed or feel like a failure. Personal circumstances can vary greatly from person to person, and we are talking about a powerful enemy - fear - that we must not underestimate.

In which cases should personal experiments not be carried out?

There are times when personal experimentation should be avoided - for example, if the patient in question has a medically diagnosed illness (such as heart disease or asthma) that is aggravated by excitement or exercise.

If an asthmatic does a personal experiment, it may have a counterproductive effect - instead of proving that panic is safe, it may encourage the patient to believe that panic is dangerous. Basically, if you are in any doubt, consult your family doctor and follow his advice.

When should you stop doing personal experiments?

The simple answer is: when you've learned everything you need to know about panic. There is no need to continue experimenting for months.

The experiments are not intended to be an end in themselves - they are intended to help those affected learn certain important facts about panic. Once that is done, no further experimentation is required. One can then confidently close this chapter and turn to other things.

What degree of healing is possible?

Complete healing is possible. But what does "complete healing" mean? It does not mean that the person will never have a panic attack in the future. If that were the goal of therapy, then there is a problem - namely, that the patient is still afraid of panic attacks.

People who are completely cured by my definition are no longer afraid of panic attacks, and if they have an occasional panic attack then that doesn't bother them. You may experience panic and anxiety at times when exposed to difficult, stressful situations for an extended period of time. This is perfectly normal; Experience has shown that such phases pass quickly if those concerned do not attach too much importance to them and do not interpret them as a "relapse". They are uncomfortable but harmless. They can also disappear completely over time.

What if I've done everything in this book and I'm still not getting better?

If a patient has carefully followed everything in this book and still sees no improvement, then he should no longer continue the exercises described - there is no point in trying "your head against the wall." Always consult with your doctor before trying the experiments and discuss the results and how you should proceed.

Please note the following:

- The patient must really face their fear of dying, going insane, or whatever it is. If he avoids this fear, however subtle it may be, then he has not done the exercises correctly and cannot expect a complete cure.

- The patient has to do the exercises until he really sees what is happening. There's no point just dipping your toes in the water. For example, if someone walks into a crowd just once, they haven't really engaged in the exercise program.

- If the patient does all of the exercises without ever having a panic attack, they may learn that the exercises are safe - but they do not learn that panic attacks are also safe. If he ever has a panic attack in the future, he will likely be upset. So, it's about facing panic attacks, not the activities or places that can trigger panic attacks.

- If those affected try to trigger a panic attack - say, by getting into a crowd - they have to remain in the corresponding situation long enough for the panic attack to develop and then subside again. Five minutes will usually not be enough - you have to reckon with about an hour.

- You have to have patience; one should not expect an "overnight cure". The hope of an instant miracle cure is a trap for the patient.

- Those affected should not interpret a possible setback as a sign that the problem-solving approach has failed in their case. Setbacks are normal. There will be setbacks. If you've had a setback, it doesn't mean you failed.

Chapter 17: The most important things in a nutshell

This is the summary of the most important points of this book again.

- A panic attack is the body's normal fear response. The fear response is a potential that everyone has. It is usually triggered in the event of a dangerous situation and enables us to react quickly and appropriately to the danger. The fear reaction is triggered randomly when a person has panic attacks for the first time.

- However, those affected do not know that. They believe that something really bad is happening to them because the fear response is accompanied by such violent sensations.

- The fear response is usually caused by stress, crises, or significant changes in someone's life that occurred within the nine months before the first panic attack.

- People do not usually realize that there is a connection between these stresses and their first panic attacks.

- Since those affected do not see the real reason for their panic attacks, they become very afraid of further attacks and of what might happen to them during these attacks.

- This fear changes them. They are oversensitive to all feelings that are somehow reminiscent of panic, and in their efforts to prevent panic attacks or to fight them as they arise, they are too preoccupied with their own feelings.

The quest to avoid panic attacks changes and narrows people's lives. It costs them a lot of time and energy to take precautionary measures and avoid feelings of panic.

- Those affected are basically the same people as before but are so seized by their own fear that their personality seems to change. However, once they understand what is happening to them and lose their fear of fear, they can go back to being what they were before.

Why panic patients are normal

Panic patients do not suffer from any mental illness - they are perfectly normal people because

- the first panic attacks have a specific, logical reason (stress, crises);

- the fear response (which is identical to a panic attack) is a potential that is common to all people;

- The reason panic attacks can recur over a long period of time is that those affected do not know enough about panic attacks and are guided by false beliefs that lead to avoidance strategies;

- The level of fear with which people will react to something that is harmless in the eyes of other people (e.g. crowds or palpitations) is quite appropriate given the fact that people think panic symptoms are dangerous. They react to danger just as a healthy person should.

The main problem is that those affected mistakenly believe panic is dangerous. This can be remedied by

- correct information and
- personal corrective experiences.

Restoration and rebuilding

Once people begin to understand the fear response, their panic attacks no longer seem confusing and illogical. Suddenly everything makes sense. Panic brings a lot of suffering and pain; the life of those affected revolves (almost exclusively) around panic and fear. It is possible to overcome that and break out of the frightening vicious circle. One can learn to lead a normal life again and cope with everyday tasks; however, there will be a lot of catching up to do. During the years when people focused on (or avoided) their panic attacks, they have often missed a lot. Fortunately, her problem does not affect her mental abilities - they will survive even the worst panic attacks completely unscathed. Concentration, memory, serenity - none of this is lost, it is only temporarily suppressed by fear and returns completely back.

Panic attacks if left to their natural course, subside on their own.

I am hopeful that you will have a complete recovery with the Help of Allaah. Always ask for Help from Allaah alone.

Bibliography

When Panic Attacks: The New, Drug-Free Anxiety Therapy That Can Change Your Life by David D. Burns M.D.

Dare: The New Way to End Anxiety and Stop Panic Attacks by Barry McDonagh

Hope and Help for Your Nerves: End Anxiety Now by Claire Weekes

Rewire Your Anxious Brain: How to Use the Neuroscience of Fear to End Anxiety, Panic, and Worry Paperback by Catherine M. Pittman

Worry Trick: How Your Brain Tricks You Into Expecting the Worst and What You Can Do About It by David A. Carbonell